Lydia Dunford-Anderson is an Associate Solicitor in Boyes Turner's Education team. She advises on all aspects of the Education, Health and Care Plan process and represents clients at the SEND Tribunal, including Health and Social Care extended appeals, case managing them from initial instructions to the appeal concluding and beyond. Lydia is acknowledged in Legal 500 and has been ranked in Chamber and Partners for the past three years inclusive (2022 – 2024) where she is noted as an 'Associate to watch'.

Lydia has written an in-depth article looking at the evolution of Education Otherwise Than At School (EOTAS), previously published on Snap Care's website and a further version published on Autism Eye's online magazine. She is a member of the Law Society and Education Law Association.

A Practical Guide to Education Otherwise Than at School or College (EOTAS/C)

A Practical Guide to Education Otherwise Than at School or College (EOTAS/C)

Lydia Dunford-Anderson
Associate Solicitor, Boyes Turner LLP
LLB (Hons) PGDip(LPC)

Law Brief Publishing

Published 2025 by Law Brief Publishing, an imprint of Law Brief Publishing Ltd
30 The Parks
Minehead
Somerset
TA24 8BT

www.lawbriefpublishing.com

Paperback: 978-1-916698-74-1

I would like to dedicate this book to
the people who put others before themselves and
strive to make education accessible to all.

PREFACE

This guide for legal practitioners on Education Otherwise Than At School/College (EOTAS/C) addresses a niche, but potentially complex, area of Special Educational Needs and/or Disability (SEND) law.

My aim is to provide a detailed overview of the legal requirements and updates through case law, and to serve as a useful resource for advising parents of children and young people with Education, Health and Care Plans (EHCPs) about EOTAS/C and the practical, as well as legal, considerations.

Much has developed in the legal world since the implementation of the Children and Families Act 2014, and the application of EOTAS/C in the proceeding ten years has been varied to say the least. This guide considers how the legal definition of EOTAS/C under the previous legislation, the Education Act 1996, compares with the current one, something that has also been examined in tribunal judgements. Examples of what EOTAS/C is not, the scope and type of evidence needed to support EOTAS/C, and how EOTAS/C links in with EHCPs are examined as well.

I would like to take this opportunity to thank my wonderful and supportive husband, family, and friends, who know I have been writing this for many an evening, and whose kind words and encouragement have been immeasurable. Thank you also to my boss for checking in and backing me throughout this process.

The law stated in this guide is believed to be correct and up-to-date as of 14 February 2025.

Lydia Dunford-Anderson
February 2025

CONTENTS

CHAPTER ONE

INTRODUCTION – DOESN'T EDUCATION HAVE TO BE IN A SCHOOL OR COLLEGE?

In short, no. Children and young people of compulsory school age (between five - sixteen)[1] can legally be educated outside of an official and registered school or college setting. One of the (arguably) most interesting and potentially litigious reasons for how this might happen is the focus of this guide.

Let us consider the huge changes that have left an impact on the education system following the COVID-19 pandemic. During the national lockdowns, many pupils were no longer able to go to school or college and, instead, taught at home. For some, this change from a formal learning environment to a more individualised set-up worked well. For others, it was harder and proved a challenge. As schools and colleges reopened to more pupils, some then found this transition difficult; some, more than three years after the last national lockdown restrictions were lifted, have continued to struggle. These pupils remain out of (at least) full-time school or college, and the success of their learning and progress are dependent on several factors. One such factor is if that child or young person has special educational needs and/or disabilities (SEND).

Under the remit of SEND law (itself part of education law), this guide will focus on the concept of Education Otherwise Than at School/College (EOTAS/C); a broad title for a niche and potentially complex area as we will go on to examine.

---

1 Section 8(1)–(3) Education Act 1996

Essentially, but not always simply, as we will explore further on, the aim of this process of EOTAS/C is for a child or young person with SEND to be taught and educationally provided for at least predominantly outside of a school or college. The legal requirements and steps to secure such an arrangement require careful consideration and understanding, which will be considered throughout this guide.

One key requirement is that the child or young person in question must have an Education, Health and Care Plan (EHCP). This a legally binding document maintained by the local authority, where the child or young person primarily resides in.[2] This EHCP must include eleven sections (A – K inclusive). The key ones for our purpose in this guide are the sections that set out a child or young person's special educational needs (section B), the provision required to meet those needs (section F), and the name and or type of educational setting (school or college) they will attend (section I). There is also the section that details funding arrangements for the special educational provision, should this be arranged through parents/a third party (section J). These four sections of EHCPs will be considered in greater detail in chapters two and four, as they are central to the concept of EOTAS/C and so sufficient attention must be given to them.

EOTAS/C offers alternative options for what information goes into an EHCP, and in which specific sections. This provides a reconsideration of the legal requirements around EHCPs, as well as the information and evidence needed to successfully inform and implement these. As will be set out, there are many stages of the EOTAS/C process where difficulties and disputes can arise. Therefore, having a sufficient knowledge of the law and potential issues is essential in being able to advise on the legal process.

The guide will cover the lifespan of the legal concept of EOTAS/C to provide a comprehensive understanding specifically for practitioners in

2 Section 24 Children and Families Act 2014

SEND law. Legal practitioners who specialise in other areas of education law may also find this, or at least specific chapters, informative, to supplement their own knowledge.

Before we examine EOTAS/C, as the focus of this guide, we must first address SEND law in the necessary detail; without such understanding it would be difficult and impractical to fully comprehend the specifics and potential complications of EOTAS/C and the relationship this concept has with EHCPs.

CHAPTER TWO

OUR STARTING POINT – PUPILS WITH SPECIAL EDUCATIONAL NEEDS AND/OR DISABILITIES (SEND)

a) Section 20 Children and Families Act 2014

We will start by setting out the definition of SEND under the existing legislation, now ten years old which followed a major review of SEND law:

> *(1) A child or young person has special educational needs if he or she has a learning difficulty or disability which calls for special educational provision to be made for him or her.*
>
> *(2) A child of compulsory school age or a young person has a learning difficulty or disability if he or she—*
>
> *(a) has a significantly greater difficulty in learning than the majority of others of the same age, or*
>
> *(b) has a disability which prevents or hinders him or her from making use of facilities of a kind generally provided for others of the same age in mainstream schools or mainstream post-16 institutions.*
>
> *(3) A child under compulsory school age has a learning difficulty or disability if he or she is likely to be within subsection (2) when of compulsory school age (or would be likely, if no special educational provision were made).*

This definition therefore covers children from birth (under compulsory school age) through to at least age sixteen, noting the compulsory school age is between five – sixteen years. Young people as a definition are generally classed up until someone turns eighteen years old i.e., younger than nineteen but over the compulsory school age.[3]

However, as will be set out in this guide, young people as a term can now apply to those up to, and including, the age of twenty-five. For our purpose, this is specifically considering young people with SEND. The implications on expanding educational support and provision for a wider range of young people will be addressed in Chapter Three.

The SEND Code of Practice 2015 provides a helpful overview of local authority responsibilities and considerations for young people aged 19-25:

> "*...to consider the need for EHC needs assessments, prepare EHC plans where needed, and maintain and review them, including the duty to ensure that all reviews of EHC plans from Year 9 (age 13-14) onwards include a focus on preparing for adulthood and, for 19-25 year olds, to have regard to whether educational or training outcomes specified in the EHC plan have been achieved*"[4]

Additional guidance confirms:

> "*...a local authority must not cease an EHC plan simply because a young person is aged 19 or over...However, this position does not mean that there is an automatic entitlement to continued support at age 19 or an expectation that those with an EHC plan should all remain in education until age 25...judgements on when to stop or maintain a*

3 Section 579(1) Education Act 1996

4 Paragraph 8.3 SEND Code of Practice 2015

plan must be made on a case-by-case basis and in accordance with the statutory tests and processes…"[5]

Going back to Section 20, another point to be aware of is the reference to "*institutions*" at (2) (b), which is defined as:

(1) *…"school" means an educational institution…providing –*

(a) *Primary education*

(b) *Secondary education, or*

(c) *Both primary and secondary education…*[6]

A useful summary of practical points to consider in line with this definition was set out by Upper Tribunal Judge Rowley in *NN v Cheshire East Council* (SEN)[7]:

"In MA v Borough of Kensington and Chelsea (SEN) [2015] UKUT 0186 (AAC) Upper Tribunal Judge Levenson decided that ***whether an entity is an educational institution*** *of one of the types listed in section 4* ***is a question of fact*** *for the specialist tribunal, taking account of all the* ***relevant evidence*** *including…those factors set out by Upper Tribunal Judge Lane in paragraph 33 of TB v Essex County Council (SEN) [2013] UKUT 0534 (AAC), namely:* ***regulation, governance, financing and administration."***[8]

I have highlighted, in my view, the key points to be aware of. This summary, and definition, will be important to remember for chapter five,

---

5 Paragraph 1 SEND: 19- to 25-year-olds' entitlement to EHC plans, 21 February 2017

6 Section 4(1) Education Act 1996

7 [2021] UKUT 220 (AAC)

8 Paragraph 26 [2021] UKUT 220 (AAC)

as it provides a central point of debate in respect of EOTAS/C and the location for this.

b) Section 21 Children and Families Act 2014 – special educational provision

Going back to the Children and Families Act 2014, a key part of the legal definition for SEND is the term "*special educational provision*", which itself is defined as follows:

> *(1) "Special educational provision", for a child aged two or more or a young person, means educational or training provision that is additional to, or different from, that made generally for others of the same age in—*
>
> *(a) mainstream schools in England,*
>
> *(b) maintained nursery schools in England,*
>
> *(c) mainstream post-16 institutions in England, or*
>
> *(d) places in England at which relevant early years education is provided.*
>
> *(2) "Special educational provision", for a child aged under two, means educational provision of any kind.*

Whilst children under five years old can receive special educational provision, for our purpose we will only be considering situations when a child is at least five years old i.e., when they are legally required to attend school, through to young people aged twenty-five years old. The simple reason for this is because the twenty-year span provides us with different periods of education and development that all happen through a child and young person's school and, if applicable, college career. Therefore, this covers all the likely potential stages when EOTAS/C may be a requirement.

This is not to say that children under the age of five are precluded from requiring EOTAS (note the term here is not EOTAS/C given the "C" stands for college), as each case will require advice on its individual merits and limitations. Arguably, however, it is less likely given their limited experience of attending educational settings full-time prior starting at a primary school, and so less chance to ascertain if EOTAS is necessary for them.

Another point to take note of, as will be addressed in chapter four, is when special educational provisions are required i.e., to facilitate education or training:

> "*A provision may be educational without itself educating a child. The word means 'of, pertaining to, or concerned with education' to quote the Oxford Shorter English Dictionary (fifth edition).*"[9]

This term is one we will come across frequently in examining EOTAS/C. It is also important to understand how central special educational provisions are in respect of EHCPs more widely.

---

9 Upper Tribunal Judge Jacobs, Paragraph 9 EAM v East Sussex County Council UA-2022-000328-HS / [2022] UKUT 193 (AAC)

CHAPTER THREE

EDUCATION, HEALTH AND CARE PLANS (EHCPs)

Speaking of EHCPs, the Children and Families Act 2014 and SEND Regulations 2014, respectively, marked a significant shift in the legal processes and requirements for supporting pupils with SEND. Set out within Part 3 of the Act, the main changes being the inclusion of young people now classed up to the age of twenty-five who can be eligible for educational provision to meet their SEND and, a main aspect of this guide, the introduction of EHCPs.

As mentioned in chapter one, EHCPs are legally binding documents issued and maintained by a child or young person's home local authority under Section 37 (1) (a) and (b) Children and Families Act 2014. Made up of Sections A – K inclusive (although local authorities have been known to add a Section L, and sometimes beyond), the basic aim of EHCPs is to meet a pupil's education, health and care needs and, in most cases, name either a specific or type of educational institution that that pupil will attend.

Chapter four addresses the relevant educational sections of EHCPs for our purpose, as previously noted, in greater detail, namely sections B, F, I. The fourth section (J) that can be relevant when EOTAS/C is involved, and the details of this will also be considered in chapter four.

Let us now examine the relevant sections of the Children and Families Act 2014 and what is set out in respect of EHCPs.

a) Section 37 (2) and (3) Children and Families Act 2014

In summary:

> *(2) …*
>
> *(a) the child's or young person's special educational needs;*
>
> *(b) the outcomes…;*
>
> *(c) the special educational provision…;*
>
> *(d) any health care provision…;*
>
> *(e) in the case of a child or a young person aged under 18, any social care provision…as a result of section 2 of the Chronically Sick and Disabled Persons Act 1970…;*
>
> *(f) any social care provision reasonably required…to the extent that the provision is not already specified in the plan under paragraph (e).*
>
> *(3) other health care and social care provision reasonably required…*

The above covers sections B – H, inclusive, of an EHCP. Concerning special educational provision detailed within Section F specifically, the respective local authority has a statutory duty to: "…*secure the specified special educational provision for the child or young person*"[10] whom it: "…*maintains an EHC plan for…*"[11]. Such a duty remains unless the child or young person's parent makes: "*suitable alternative arrangements*"[12] for their education, and we shall consider this in chapter six.

---

10 Section 42(2) & (6) Children and Families Act 2014

11 Section 42(1) Children and Families Act 2014

12 Section 42(5) Children and Families Act 2014

For the outstanding EHCP sections, we need to also look at the SEND Regulations 2014.

b) Regulation 12 (1) and (4) SEND Regulations 2014

Sections A, I, J and K respectively are addressed in regulation 12 (1) and (4) SEND Regulations 2014 along with the other above sections. Consideration must therefore be given to both the Act and Regulations although, in practice, the Regulations arguably provide a more accessible point of reference. Whilst still not concise, the format and language appear clearer, mainly due to the inclusion of all sections of an EHCP and specific references to these:

> *12.—(1) …*
>
> *(a) the views, interests and aspirations of the child and his parents or the young person (section A);*
>
> *(b) the child or young person's special educational needs (section B);*
>
> *(c) the child or young person's health care needs which relate to their special educational needs (section C);*
>
> *(d) the child or young person's social care needs which relate to their special educational needs or to a disability (section D);*
>
> *(e) the outcomes sought for him or her (section E);*
>
> *(f) the special educational provision required by the child or young person (section F);*
>
> *(g) any health care provision reasonably required by the learning difficulties or disabilities which result in the child or young person having special educational needs (section G);*

> *(h) (i) any social care provision which must be made for the child or young person as a result of section 2 of the Chronically Sick and Disabled Persons Act 1970 (section H1);*
>
> *(ii) any other social care provision reasonably required by the learning difficulties or disabilities which result in the child or young person having special educational needs (section H2);*
>
> *(i). the name of the school, maintained nursery school, post-16 institution or other institution to be attended by the child or young person and the type of that institution or, where the name of a school or other institution is not specified in the EHC plan, the type of school or other institution to be attended by the child or young person (section I); and*
>
> *(j) where any special educational provision is to be secured by a direct payment, the special educational needs and outcomes to be met by the direct payment (section J),*
>
> …
>
> *(4) The advice and information obtained…must be set out in appendices to the EHC plan (section K).*

The Regulations provide a very useful resource; the list should be considered in the order written when examining against an EHCP.

As well as the Act and Regulations, an accompanying SEND Code of Practice was initially published on 1 September 2014 with a revised version issued in January 2015; it is the latter that we shall now examine, as this is the version referred to in practice.

c) Paragraph 9.69 SEND Code of Practice 2015

A detailed summary of all EHCP sections is provided in chapter nine at paragraph 9.69. Extra information and guidance are set out for each section in a table format for easy comparison. The context is very useful, and below is the information provided for the educational sections we will be focusing on in chapter five of this guide. Note that the text in bold is as written in the Code of Practice and so kept in for continuity:

Section (B)

- *All of the child or young person's identified special educational needs* ***must*** *be specified*
- *SEN may include needs for health and social care provision that are treated as special educational provision because they educate or train the child or young person*

Section (F)

- *Provision* ***must*** *be detailed and specific and should normally be quantified, for example, in terms of the type, hours and frequency of support and level of expertise, including where this support is secured through a Personal Budget*
- *Provision* ***must*** *be specified for each and every need specified in section B. It should be clear how the provision will support achievement of the outcomes*
- *Where health or social care provision educates or trains a child or young person, it* ***must*** *appear in this section*
- *There should be clarity as to how advice and information gathered has informed the provision specified. Where the local authority has*

departed from that advice, they should say so and give reasons for it

- *In some cases, flexibility will be required to meet the changing needs of the child or young person including flexibility in the use of a Personal Budget*

- *The plan should specify:*

    - *any appropriate facilities and equipment, staffing arrangements and curriculum*

    - *any appropriate modifications to the application of the National Curriculum, where relevant*

    - *any appropriate exclusions from the application of the National Curriculum or the course being studied in a post-16 setting, in detail, and the provision which it is proposed to substitute for any such exclusions in order to maintain a balanced and broadly based curriculum o where residential accommodation is appropriate, that fact*

    - *where there is a Personal Budget, the outcomes to which it is intended to contribute (detail of the arrangements for a Personal Budget, including any direct payment,* **must** *be included in the plan and these should be set out in section J)*

Section (I)

- *The name and type of the school, maintained nursery school, post-16 institution or other institution to be attended by the child or young person and the type of that institution (or, where the name of a school or other institution is not specified in the EHC plan, the type of school or other institution to be attended by the child or young person)*

- *These details* ***must*** *be included only in the final EHC plan, not the draft EHC plan sent to the child's parent or to the young person*

Section (J)

- This section should provide detailed information on any Personal Budget that will be used to secure provision in the EHC plan

- It should set out the arrangements in relation to direct payments as required by education…regulations

- The special educational needs and outcomes that are to be met by any direct payment **must** be specified

It is recommended to refer to these descriptions when we examine the relationship between EHCPs and EOTAS/C in chapter five.

Chapter nine of the Code of Practice also provides guidance specifically on EHCP preparation, not just about the content of the sections, as noted above. For example: "*EHC plans should be clear, concise, understandable and accessible to parents, children, young people, providers and practitioners. They should be written so they can be understood by professionals in any local authority.*"[13] As EHCPs are documents that are referred to by various educational staff, therapists and other experts, potentially across multiple local authority boroughs if a child or young person moves house, the wording needs to accommodate all these readers.

The idea of unambiguous wording is also central to setting out EOTAS/C provision when, as we will examine further on in chapters five

[13] Paragraph 9.61 SEND Code of Practice 2015

and eleven respectively, there are likely to be a potentially wide range of professionals involved in delivering the provision.

Now that we have an overview of the educational sections of an EHCP, and an understanding of how important detail and clarity of the wording across all sections are, we can focus on the main topic of this guide; EOTAS/C.

CHAPTER FOUR

EOTAS/C

a) What is EOTAS/C?

The legal definition is set out under Section 61 of the Children and Families Act 2014 as follows:

> (1) *A local authority in England may arrange for any special educational provision that it has decided is necessary for a child or young person for whom it is responsible to be*
>
> *made otherwise than in a school....*
>
> (2) *An authority may do so only if satisfied that it would be* *inappropriate* (emphasis added) *for the provision to be made in a school...*
>
> (3) *Before doing so, the authority must consult the child's parent or the young person.*

Whilst reference is only given to schools, the same principle applies to colleges as these are institutions that also deliver education, specifically secondary education, as per the definition and guidance noted in chapter two of this guide. The Upper Tribunal in *NN v Cheshire East Council* (SEN)[14] confirmed: "*The relevant provisions of the Children and Families Act 2014 also refer to education otherwise than at a post-16 institution...*"[15]

---

[14] HS/260/2021 / [2021] UKUT 220 (AAC)

[15] HS/260/2021 Paragraph 2 footnote 1 / [2021] UKUT 220 (AAC)

Ahead of considering the Section 61 definition in further detail, it is useful to compare it with previous legalisation, the Education Act 1996, as there are similarities and slight, but arguably interesting, changes in wording:

(1) *Where a local authority are satisfied that it would be* *inappropriate* (emphasis added) *for-*

(a) the special educational provision which a learning difficulty of a child in their area calls for, or

(b) any part of such provision,

to be made in a school, they may arrange for the provision (or, as the case may be, for part of it) to be made otherwise than in a school.

(2) Before making an arrangement under this section, a local authority shall consult the child's parent.[16]

The legal definition has remained fairly unaltered across the two statutes, with the key word (emphasised above) being "*inappropriate*"; this will be examined in later in this chapter.

Before doing so, there is a difference to note in the wording of (1) in the Children and Families Act 2014 and (1)(b) of the Education Act 1996 respectively. The former addresses "*any special educational provision*", with the latter detailing "*any part of such* (special educational) *provision*". This distinction is interesting, as the Education Act 1996 wording seems to acknowledge that aspects, but not necessarily all, of a special educational provision may be appropriately delivered within a school or college setting. The current definition, on the other hand, does not

16 Section 319 Education Act 1996

specifically outline this. Upper Tribunal Judge Rowley considered this in *N v Cheshire East* (SEN)[17].

The concept of distinguishing between provisions which would be appropriate, or not, to be delivered within a school or college, and the impact this has on EHCPs, is examined in greater detail in chapter eleven.

Furthermore, *M & M v West Sussex County Council (SEN)* noted that:

> "*While the predecessor legislation about statements of SEN, contained in Part IV of the Education Act 1996, expressly provided for a placement of 'education otherwise than in school' the Children and Families Act 2014 ("2014 Act") does not. However, the 2014 Act regime is not blind to the possibility that a child with an EHC Plan might not always be appropriately educated in a school.*"[18]

Focusing back on this Section 61 definition in the "*2014 Act*", the requirements for EOTAS/C are, on initial reading, simple:

(1) a child or young person's home local authority to confirm special educational provision required outside of a school (or college)

(2) such provision to only be secured as per (1) if it is otherwise inappropriate to be delivered in either type of setting (i.e., a school or college)

(3) the parents of the child, or young person themself, must be consulted about this option before implementing

Taking (1): special educational provision has already been covered in chapter two, as has the definition of a school or college. (2) provides us

17 Paragraphs 29-30 HS/260/2021 / [2021] UKUT 220 (AAC)

18 Paragraph 2 HS/2370/2017 / [2018] UKUT 347 (AAC)

with a central concept of EOTAS/C; "*inappropriate*", which we will examine in greater detail. Finally, (3) is clear about the action required from the local authority, and chapter nine considers the importance of parental or young person views in this respect.

Here, we will now address the key principle of the legal definition of EOTAS/C; "*inappropriate*".

b) "*Appropriate*" vs "*Inappropriate*"

An initial examination of relevant legislation under Section 14 of the Education Act 1996 provides us with reference to "*appropriate*":

> (1) *A local authority shall secure…sufficient schools for providing-*
>
> (a) *primary education, and*
>
> (b) *education that is secondary…,*
>
> *Are available for their area.*
>
> (2) *…schools…shall not be regarded as sufficient for the purposes of subsection (1) unless they are sufficient in number, character and equipment to provide for all pupils the opportunity of appropriate education.*
>
> (3) *In subsection (1) "appropriate education" means education which offers such variety and training as may be desirable in the view of-*
>
> (a) *the pupils' different ages, abilities and aptitudes…"*

The key wording is at 3(a) and requires specific consideration.

There is ambiguity here in that pupils' SEN is not specifically addressed. 3(a) could be seen to cover this under "*abilities*", but it is interesting that "*needs*" is not directly included as a criterion. If we compare with a section from the Children and Families Act, for example:

> (4) … (a) *the school or other institution requested is unsuitable for the age, ability, aptitude or special educational needs of the child or young person concerned…*"

SEN is clearly set out as an individual consideration when addressing potential school or college placements; why such distinction is not provided for under the Education Act 1996 is unclear.

Focusing now on the main question for EOTAS/C of if it is inappropriate for special educational provision to be delivered within an educational institution, we turn to case law considering a Statement of SEN, the EHCP predecessor, and so under the Section 319 Education Act 1996 definition. The scope of reasoning to apply when considering "*inappropriateness*" of provision remains valid, informative and thought-provoking:

> "*…it is not enough for the local education authority to ask simply "can" the school meet the statement of needs… To confine the question thus does not…give proper scope to…the words "are satisfied that it would be inappropriate for… the special educational provision which a child calls for…to be made in a school."…in…answering that question, if a local education authority is to give full effect to the word "inappropriate", it has to see if a school would "not be suitable" or "would not be proper… the local education authority has to take into account all the circumstances of the case in hand.*"[19]

This important judgement from *TM v London Borough of Hounslow* will be examined in further detail in chapter seven.

---

[19] Paragraph 26 Lord Justice Aikens, *TM v London Borough of Hounslow* C1/2008/2712 / [2009] UKUT 240 (AAC)

As you will see throughout this guide, "*suitable*" is a term frequently used within education law, and specifically within SEN. "*Proper*" is arguably interchangeable with "*suitable*", and so we will stay with the latter for our purpose.

It is important to distinguish that this is not concerning an individual school or college, but:

> "*...whether, in general, it would be inappropriate for the provision required...to be made in a school* [or college]. *The generality of the section 61 test is shown by the enactment's reference to "a school""*[20]

when applying the definition of EOTAS/C. This requires thought to, potentially, any school or college within England when determining if provision could be delivered within any such institution.

However, the Upper Tribunal in *M & M v West Sussex County Council (SEN)* speculated that:

> "*Arguably, section 61 should not be applied by reference to a notional school but by reference to the schools that a child might realistically attend.*"[21]

Chapter eight considers the categories of schools and colleges in greater detail; the range of settings allows for both broad examination and scope for opposing legal arguments in respect of EOTAS/C.

Returning to "*inappropriate*", this wording and guidance offered in *TM v London Borough of Hounslow* allows scope for each local authority to consider if the threshold has been met; the lack of a set legal definition allows for potentially limitless arguments on either side. However, the

[20] Paragraph 48 Upper Tribunal Judge Mitchell, *AA & BB v Bristol City Council* [2023] UKUT 52 (AAC)

[21] Paragraph 23 HS/2370/2017 / [2018] UKUT 347 (AAC)

absence of a clear specification, beyond comparisons to other terminology, does cause increased risk of disputes between local authorities and parents or young people; this will be examined in chapters five, seven, nine and ten respectively.

Satisfying the legal criteria for EOTAS/C therefore requires confirmation that it would be inappropriate, (and so successfully established that it would be neither "*suitable*" or "*proper*"), without a specific definition for this, for any educational provision to be delivered to a child or young person within any educational institution when considering "*...all the circumstances of the case...*"[22] Suddenly, not so simple.

What is also potentially litigious and complex is the process to then correctly detail, and so secure, EOTAS/C in an EHCP; we shall now go on to examine this.

22 Paragraph 26 Lord Justice Aikens, *TM v London Borough of Hounslow* [2009] UKUT 240 (AAC)

CHAPTER FIVE

HOW DOES EOTAS/C FIT INTO EHCPS?

We have established that there cannot be EOTAS/C without an EHCP. What must now be examined is the specific relationship of how and where EOTAS/C is detailed in an EHCP, and the requirements and legal processes to follow. As will be set out, this relationship can be complex and there have been differing judgements in case law addressing this point, allowing for contrasting arguments from parents and local authorities. This is where having an up to date and comprehensive understanding of the legal and practical link between EOTAS/C and EHCPs is vital if advising as a SEND legal practitioner.

Working our way through the educational sections of the EHCP is logical and, given that Section B needs inform provision at F, which in turn apprises placement in Section I, it makes sense to keep this order for our analysis.

Therefore, we shall start with section B – Special educational needs.

Section B – Special Educational Needs

As a refresher on what the legal requirements are for Section B of an EHCP:

Section (B)

- *All of the child or young person's identified special educational needs **must** be specified*

- *SEN may include needs for health and social care provision that are treated as special educational provision because they educate or train the child or young person*[23]

This definition allows for a wide range of needs to be depicted, dependent on the individual child or young person. Such scope is set out under the following sub-categories:

> "*Cognition and learning*
>
> *...Learning difficulties cover a wide range of needs...where children are likely to need support in all areas of the curriculum...*
>
> *Communication and interaction*
>
> *...The profile for every child with speech, language and communication needs is different...They may have difficulty with one, some or all of the different aspects of speech, language or social communication...*
>
> *Social, emotional and mental health difficulties*
>
> *...These may include becoming withdrawn or isolated...These behaviours may reflect underlying mental health difficulties...or...disorders such as attention deficit disorder, attention deficit hyperactive disorder or attachment disorder.*
>
> *Sensory and/or physical needs*
>
> *Some children and young people...have a disability which prevents or hinders them from making use of the educational facilities generally provided...Many children and young people with vision impairment...hearing impairment...or a multi-sensory impairment*

23 Paragraph 9.69 SEND Code of Practice 2015 & Regulation 12(1)(b) SEND Regulations 2014

will require specialist support and/or equipment to access their learning..."[24]

Case law has subsequently addressed examples of when Section B needs (under the above sub-categories) inform EOTAS/C as required Section F provision.

Firstly, *M v Hertfordshire County Council*[25]. The child, 'A', had both a rumination disorder and suffered with school-related anxiety. Evidence as to the severity and impact of these needs was provided by a range of professionals, but not all through formal assessments. The importance of gathering such evidence when addressing EOTAS/C will be considered in greater detail in chapter nine. Regarding A, his: "*...anxiety is such that, at the moment, he is unable to attend a place of education without endangering his emotional welfare and physical health.*"[26] The First-Tier Tribunal, however, determined that: "*...we do not accept that there is evidence that [A] is medically unfit to attend school as there is no current opinion based on a proper assessment of him by a suitably qualified professional.*"[27] The Upper Tribunal held: "*...that the First-tier Tribunal, in its approach to section 61, failed to take into account the wider school-related anxiety case...associated with vomiting...*"[28] The decision was set aside and to be re-determined by the First-Tier Tribunal.

Whilst it may seem arguable that special educational provision would be inappropriately delivered within a school or college in these

---

24 Paragraphs 6.28 – 6.35 SEND Code of Practice 2015

25 [2019] UKUT 37 (AAC)

26 [2019] UKUT 37 (AAC) paragraph 19 referencing "*The professional evidence before the First-tier Tribunal*"

27 [2019] UKUT 37 (AAC) paragraph 42 referencing paragraph 33 of the First Tier Tribunal decision

28 [2019] UKUT 37 (AAC) paragraph 44

circumstances, subsequent case law has echoed the reasoning in *M v Hertfordshire.*

AA & BB v Bristol City Council[29] also considered school-related anxiety, here in respect of 'R' who was in Year 5 at the time of the First-Tier Tribunal hearing and faced up to two transitions into a primary school, and then into a secondary placement. Despite R's acknowledged school-related anxiety, which was argued meant it: "*...would be inappropriate to put him through two transitions within a year...*"[30] it was decided that this anxiety: "*...was not such as to prevent it from being addressed in a school setting...*"[31] The First-Tier Tribunal went even further to determine that:

> "*A child with R's profile, who had been absent from school-based education for a time, would be more likely to make a successful transition back to such education in a primary school setting... The necessary integration into school-based learning would be absent under the "model proposed by the parents*"[32] [i.e., EOTAS/C]

Following these judgements, it is important to appreciate that school-based anxiety, as an example, does not automatically evidence a child or young person requiring EOTAS/C provision; a reminder to SEND law practitioners to: "*...take into account all the circumstances of the case in hand.*"[33]

---

29 [2023] UKUT 52 (AAC)

30 [2023] UKUT 52 (AAC) paragraph 3 referencing paragraph 152 of the First Tier Tribunal decision

31 [2023] UKUT 52 (AAC) paragraph 5 referencing paragraph 158 of the First Tier Tribunal decision

32 UA-2021-000264-HS Paragraph 7 referencing paragraph 160 of the First Tier Tribunal decision / [2023] UKUT 52 (AAC)

33 C1/2008/2712 Paragraph 26 Lord Justice Aikens, *TM v London Borough of Hounslow* C1/2008/2712 / [2009] UKUT 240 (AAC)

We now move onto how EOTAS/C is expected to be set out in Section F as special educational provision.

Section F – Special Educational Provision

Assuming that Section B of an EHCP does set out special educational needs that require EOTAS/C, and so:

> *"Provision **must** be specified for each and every need specified in section B…"*[34]

we can go on to consider how such provision is addressed in Section F. As will be examined, case law has repeatedly confirmed that provision through EOTAS/C must only be detailed within Section F of an EHCP.

We first look at *M & M v West Sussex CC* (SEN)[35], concerning 'L' who had learning difficulties and a range of needs, and: "*…was placed at risk of, and subjected to actual, sexual exploitation.*"[36] Professional evidence advocated: "*…a small caring and nurturing specialist school*"[37] for L, with prior education to be delivered at home. The Upper Tribunal held:

> "*…that the First-tier Tribunal erred in law…the tribunal gave inadequate reasons for failing to address whether some sort of provision ought to have been made in section F of L's EHC Plan for education otherwise than in a school.*"[38]

[34] Paragraph 9.69 SEND Code of Practice 2015

[35] HS/2370/2017 / [2018] UKUT 347 (AAC)

[36] HS/2370/2017 / [2018] UKUT 347 (AAC) paragraph 4

[37] HS/2370/2017 / [2018] UKUT 347 (AAC) paragraph 7 referring to "*The report of an educational psychologist, dated 28 January 2016*"

[38] HS/2370/2017 / [2018] UKUT 347 (AAC) paragraph 70

Upper Tribunal Judge Mitchell also gave general clarification that:

> "*...it is...open to a local authority or tribunal, in an appropriate case...to make section 61 provision within section F of an EHC Plan (the section setting out the required special educational provision), if...it is satisfied that the section 61(2) condition is met.*"[39]

Following this judgement was *Derbyshire County Council v EM and DM* (SEN)[40] involving two sisters with: "*...significant disabling conditions.*"[41] It was ordered by the First-Tier Tribunal: "*...for provision for 'education otherwise than in school' under section F of the sisters' education and health care plans (EHC Plan)...*"[42]

This point, as a whole, was undisputed. Other grounds of appeal centred on how to approach Section I, which we will go on to cover further on in this chapter, along with other cases addressed here.

NN v Cheshire East Council (SEN)[43] re-affirmed previous judgements and provided a very useful "*summary and guidance*"[44] that outlines key considerations and legal principles from prior case law:

> "*...The tribunal must consider section 61 CFA 2014...It must...ask whether it is satisfied that it would be inappropriate for...any special educational provision that is has decided is necessary for the child to be made in any school...the tribunal must ask if a school would 'not be suitable' or would 'not be proper'...Any special educational provision*

---

39 HS/2370/2017 / [2018] UKUT 347 (AAC) paragraph 67

40 HS/571/2019 & HS/572/2019 / [2019] UKUT 240 (AAC)

41 Paragraph 1 HS/571/2019 & HS/572/2019 / [2019] UKUT 240 (AAC)

42 Paragraph 1 HS/571/2019 & HS/572/2019 / [2019] UKUT 240 (AAC)

43 HS/260/2021 / [2021] UKUT 220 (AAC)

44 Paragraph 47 HS/260/2021 / [2021] UKUT 220 (AAC)

which will be made otherwise than in a school or type of school will be set out in Section F."[45]

As background to the case, 'W' was thirteen years old and had diagnoses of Autism and Pathological Demand Avoidance. He had only been educated at home to date, and the request from W's mother and grandmother was: "*...that W's provision should be delivered by education otherwise than at school.*'[46] The main grounds of appeal to the Upper Tribunal focused not on the Section F wording, but on that of Section I. As we will examine in chapter eleven, this case also set a precedent for a significant shift in the application of EOTAS/C alongside school or college-based provision.

DM v Cornwall County Council (SEN)[47] concerned a child with a complex profile of special educational needs including: "*...foetal alcohol spectrum disorder, autistic spectrum disorder, organic brain damage secondary to prenatal exposure to drugs...*"[48] The child's grandmother brought the appeal as his legal guardian, and was in agreement with the local authority: "*...that it was necessary for the child to be educated otherwise than in a school.*"[49]

This case, and the subsequent appeal to the Upper Tribunal, considered the legality and practical implications of Section F wording of how frequently the EOTAS/C provision was to be reviewed. The wording included through the First-Tier Tribunal appeal was: "*...subject to termly review, and until such time as it is no longer necessary for [him] to be educated in this way due to it being inappropriate for provision to be made*

---

45 Paragraph 47 a, b & HS/260/2021 / i [2021] UKUT 220 (AAC)

46 Paragraph 8 HS/260/2021 / [2021] UKUT 220 (AAC) referring to "*The predominant issue before the tribunal...*"

47 UA-2021-000606-HS / [2022] UKUT 230 (AAC)

48 UA-2021-000606-HS Paragraph 3 / [2022] UKUT 230 (AAC)

49 UA-2021-000606-HS Paragraph 4 / [2022] UKUT 230 (AAC)

in a school.'[50] The Upper Tribunal confirmed this wording was legally compliant for an EHCP:

> "*...the phrase "subject to termly review" is plainly intended to refer to termly reviews of the provision while the child is being educated otherwise than in school and does not encompass termly reviews of whether the education should continue to be otherwise than in school.*"[51]

Upper Tribunal Judge Wright went on to cite this helpful clarification from the First-Tier Tribunal's decision:

> "*...the Tribunal is settling the EHC plan for the coming year and does not need to resolve [the difference of opinion as to the length of time for which EOTAS would be necessary] as both parties agreed that is it not likely that it is appropriate for [the child] to be educated at school during the currency of this EHC plan and it is therefore necessary for him to be educated otherwise than at school.*"[52]

Such "*currency*" would conclude through: "*...an Annual Review [of this EHC plan] which will provide the opportunity for the parties to decide on the...appropriate provision at that time and into the future.*"[53]

Whilst Section F provision is generally required to be:

---

50 UA-2021-000606-HS Paragraph 9 / [2022] UKUT 230 (AAC) referring to "*...changes ordered by the tribunal to the EHCP.*"

51 UA-2021-000606-HS Paragraph 11 / [2022] UKUT 230 (AAC)

52 UA-2021-000606-HS Paragraph 12 / [2022] UKUT 230 (AAC) referring to "*...the tribunal's decision...in paragraph 8...*'

53 UA-2021-000606-HS Paragraph 12 / [2022] UKUT 230 (AAC) referring to "*...the tribunal's decision...in paragraph 8...*'

> "*...detailed and specific and should normally be quantified, for example, in terms of the type, hours and frequency of support and level of expertise...*"[54]

there is scope for: "*In some cases, flexibility...required to meet the changing needs of the child or young person.*"[55] *DM v Cornwall* relied on such flexibility in determining the level of detail required for reviewing Section F EOTAS/C provision:

> "*The tribunal was plainly alive to the fact that because the child was not being educated in a school it would be necessary for up to date feedback to be provided about his progress and experience of education... "[t]utors need flexibility to progress interventions as they go along... With [education otherwise than in school], this is a proper aspect of discretion given that it must be a dynamic and ongoing process."...the tribunal then ordered in Section F of the EHCP... "Key adults should liaise half-termly as part of a review meeting.""*[56]

The Upper Tribunal found the ordered Section F wording was sufficiently detailed, given the circumstances of the case at hand, and the First-Tier Tribunal has not acted unlawfully in deciding on such wording.

Upper Tribunal Judge Wright also commented on overall differences that may arise when considering provision both in and otherwise than in school, and how such should be specified in Section F:

> "*...in some very general sense that educational provision which is bounded by a school building and the provision and rules that may*

---

54 Paragraph 9.69 SEND Code of Practice 2015

55 Paragraph 9.69 SEND Code of Practice 2015

56 UA-2021-000606-HS Paragraphs 16–17 / [2022] UKUT 230 (AAC) referring to "*The tribunal addressed the ned for reviews in the context of 'education otherwise then in school'* at paragraphs 60–78 of its decision"

> *apply to all pupils in that school may to an extent be assumed and not need to be stated whereas that provision may need to appear more explicitly in a case where the EHCP concerns a child being educated at home and otherwise than in school.*"[57]

Whilst there is no legal requirement to include the term EOTAS/C in Section F, I would argue it is sensible to do so at the start, with all provisions listed after this to be delivered by this method. Furthermore, reference to Section 61 could also be added for additional clarity but, again, there is no legal requirement for this. The only EHCP Sections that reference statute is H1 (the Chronically Sick and Disabled Persons Act 1970, section 2). References to specific aspects of school or college-based provisions should not be in Section F if, for example, the child or young person will not be receiving any of their EOTAS/C provision within a formal classroom set-up.

The next case of note is *London Borough of Camden v KT*[58] involving 'P' who had: "*...autism, attention deficit hyperactivity disorder and dyslexia.*"[59] The local authority appealed to the Upper Tribunal on grounds including: "*...that the tribunal had no power to order education otherwise than at school (EOTAS) at all, or certainly not without the consent of the local authority.*"[60]

Upper Tribunal Judge Jacobs noted that the First-Tier Tribunal: "*...made its own assessment and came to its independent conclusion that it would be inappropriate for P's special educational provision to be made in a*

57 UA-2021-000606-HS Paragraph 7 / [2022] UKUT 230 (AAC)

58 UA-2023-000056-HS / [2023] UKUT 225 (AAC)

59 Paragraph 1 UA-2023-000056-HS / [2023] UKUT 225 (AAC)

60 Paragraph 3 UA-2023-000056-HS / [2023] UKUT 225 (AAC)

school."[61] Given that P's special educational needs and disability were undisputed:

> "*The tribunal found that this disability called for a range of provision. This provision included that it be delivered for the time being outside a school…In order for P's education to be effective, it had to be delivered at his home…*"[62]

Relevant wording was already clearly set out by the parties in Section F:

> "*…in the final version of the Working Document – the version…that the tribunal used as the basis for its decision - …P will require special educational provision to be delivered somewhere other than in a school (EOTAS).*"[63]

Therefore: "*In conclusion, on the evidence in this case, I see no objection in principle to EOTAS being included in Section F. If Ms McColgan* [local authority counsel] *was arguing that EOTAS can never have any place in Section F…I reject it.*"[64]

Guidance was also provided as to the legal application of special educational provision in respect of EOTAS/C specifically:

> "*Section 21(1) provides that special educational provision means 'educational or training provision that is additional to, or different from, that made generally for others of the same age in mainstream schools in England…By definition, a provision for a child's education*

61 Paragraph 8 UA-2023-000056-HS / [2023] UKUT 225 (AAC) referring to "*…paragraph 48 of* [the tribunal's] *written reasons*"

62 Paragraph 28 UA-2023-000056-HS / [2023] UKUT 225 (AAC)

63 Paragraph 7 UA-2023-000056-HS / [2023] UKUT 225 (AAC)

64 Paragraph 28 UA-2023-000056-HS / [2023] UKUT 225 (AAC)

> *to be delivered outside a school is different from provision generally available in schools.*"[65]

A reminder here that a local authority's duty for Section F under Section 42(2) does not extend to provide the best education for a child or young person through an EHCP; only one that is appropriate and suitable, as noted in *R v Surrey CC ex p H*[66]. Provision must be such that is reasonably required, as confirmed in *A v Hertfordshire*[67]. This is why the wording in Section F i.e., the provision to be delivered through EOTAS/C is important; if it is not clear, specific and detailed as the child's needs permit, then it makes it very difficult to understand a) what support will be provided and b) who will do so i.e., any training/experience/qualifications etc. that they need. This also makes it difficult to enforce the provision, with ultimate responsibility for this on the local authority.

Additional grounds of appeal raised by the local authority included specific Section F provisions which were only able to be delivered within a school or college, as well as submissions regarding enforceability of EOTAS/C provisions within a home environment. The examples of provisions that, in the local authority's argument, could not be delivered unless in a school or college were:

> "…'*highly structured, clear and predictable routines and boundaries and explicit instructions'…'multi-sensory teaching methods to be employed as often as possible, capitalising on visual*

---

65 Paragraphs 27 - 28 UA-2023-000056-HS / [2023] UKUT 225 (AAC)

66 (1984) 83 LGR 219

67 [2006] EWHC 3428; (2007) ELR 95

methods'...techniques that must be used by 'Staff working with 'P'...within a group and individually'."[68]

The Upper Tribunal held that all Section F provision quoted did not require a school (or college) to deliver these. Referring to the first and second provisions, staring with "*...highly structured...*" and "*...multi-sensory teaching...*" respectively, Upper Tribunal Judge Jacobs commented: "*I see no reason why either of those refers to provision in a school. Both are equally applicable regardless of context.*"[69] On the third, "*...techniques that must be used by 'Staff...'*", these were: *...equally applicable outside a school. A few infelicitous words in over five pages of provisions in Section F is not sufficient to make* [Ms McColgan's] *argument good in the context of consistent statements that the tribunal was relying on section 61.*"[70]

As to the matter of enforceability of EOTAS/C provision within Section F, the distinction was highlighted between a local authority's statutory duty under Section 42(2) to: "*...secure the specified special educational provision for the child or young person*"[71] whom it: "*...maintains an EHC plan for...*"[72] and Section 42(5) which enables parents to make their own arrangements for their child's education, provided these are: "*...suitable alternative arrangements.*"[73] In the latter, the local authority is relieved of their legal obligation under Section 42(2).

London Borough of Camden v KT reasoned that Section 42(5) was to be considered ahead of Section 42(2), meaning the onus would initially fall

---

68 Paragraph 10 UA-2023-000056-HS / [2023] UKUT 225 (AAC) referring to submissions from Ms McColgan, local authority counsel

69 Paragraph 10 UA-2023-000056-HS / [2023] UKUT 225 (AAC)

70 Paragraph 10 UA-2023-000056-HS / [2023] UKUT 225 (AAC)

71 Section 42(2) & (6) Children and Families Act 2014

72 Section 42(1) Children and Families Act 2014

73 Section 42(5) Children and Families Act 2014

on KT (parent to P) to make such arrangements for P's education out of school:

> "*The local authority did not impose EOTAS on KT, nor did the First-tier Tribunal. It was KT who argued for the provision and the tribunal accepted her argument. She could, of course, refuse to provide the provision…if she were to do so, the plan would have to be revised and different provision ordered.*"[74]

I take issue with this reasoning, as requesting EOTAS/C to be secured and delivered through an EHCP does not legally require initial confirmation if the child or young person's parent can deliver such provision. EHCPs are a local authority's, not parental, legal responsibility to make and maintain, as noted in Ms McColgan's skeleton argument: "*…an FtT…has no power to impose obligations on parents via an EHC Plan.*"[75] This point was accepted by the Upper Tribunal, along with: "*…EOTAS being included in Section F…*", and so it is unclear why the question of if KT could provide such provision was even considered, irrespective of if she had offered to do so. I would be cautious of applying such reasoning, or, and only if advisable in the circumstances, to instead have any additional provision/s a parent is content to deliver out of school or college separately recorded, thus ensuring the local authority remains solely liable for the entirety of Section F of the EHCP. Ideally though, I would want to avoid such a situation, given the potential legal complications and disputes that could arise over EOTAS/C provision responsibility.

We shall now look at the, arguably, most ambiguous EHCP Section when considering EOTAS/C; Section I placement and/or type of placement.

---

[74] Paragraph 31 UA-2023-000056-HS / [2023] UKUT 225 (AAC)

[75] Paragraph 32 referring to paragraph 57 of Ms McColgan's skeleton argument UA-2023-000056-HS / [2023] UKUT 225 (AAC)

Section I - Placement name and/or type

Case law has examined the wording of the Children and Families Act 2014, with notable gaps open for interpretation and a subsequent lack of certainty on how to address the relationship between EOTAS/C and Section I. As will be examined, judgements have varied over the ten years since the Children and Families Act became law.

A reminder on what this legislation sets out for Section I:

> *"The name and type of the school, maintained nursery school, post-16 institution or other institution to be attended by the child or young person and the type of that institution (or, where the name of a school or other institution is not specified in the EHC plan, the type of school or other institution to be attended by the child or young person)"*[76]

As this does not specifically provide reference to EHCPs concerning EOTAS/C, case law has attempted to clarify this.

First, *East Sussex County Council v TW*[77] which concerned 'T' who had social, emotional and mental health needs including autism and attention deficit hyperactivity disorder. Within the Upper Tribunal grounds of appeal included clarification on whether Section I could name either Brighton and Sussex Care Ltd (BASC) and, or, T's home. The First-Tier Tribunal had decided that both could be included. The Upper Tribunal, however, dismissed the reasoning on both points, and confirmed:

> *"...Section I must contain the name or type of institution 'to be attended by' the person...The phrase 'supported living provided by Brighton and Sussex Care Ltd'...does not identify something that Theo can attend...Theo's home is where he lives...It does not fit into the*

[76] Paragraph 9.69 SEND Code of Practice 2015 & Sections 39-40 Children and Families Act 2014

[77] HS/1906/2016 / [2016] UKUT 0528 (AAC)

> *language used by regulation 12(1)(i), which deals with just the type of school or institution that must be inappropriate in order for section 61 to apply…*"[78]

The Upper Tribunal also clarified that Section I cannot include additional information to pre-empt a placement breaking down; it is only to detail: "*…the name or type of institution 'to be attended by' the young person.*"[79]

We return to *M & M v West Sussex County Council* (SEN)[80], where the Upper Tribunal had to consider the legal requirements under Sections 39-40 Children and Families Act 2014 for local authorities to name a placement and/or type in situations when no such placement was appropriate. The decision from *East Sussex County Council v TW* was not disputed and confirmed here that L's home could not be named in Section I, given it was not an educational institution. Upper Tribunal Judge Mitchell also reaffirmed that:

> "*The First-tier Tribunal could not…have materially erred in law by failing to address whether 'education otherwise than at school' should have been specified in section I of L's EHC Plan.*"[81]

The question remained as to what wording could, and indeed should, go into Section I to satisfy Sections 39-40. Two options were presented:

> "*…the ultimate aim of making it appropriate for a child to be educated in a school…or as part of an educational package involving*

---

78 HS/1906/2016 Paragraphs 32-33 / [2016] UKUT 0528 (AAC)

79 HS/1906/2016 Paragraph 32 / [2016] UKUT 0528 (AAC)

80 HS/2370/2017 / [2018] UKUT 347 (AAC)

81 HS/2370/2017 Paragraph 66 / [2018] UKUT 347 (AAC)

elements of attendance at a school and education otherwise than in a school..."[82]

The former seems presumptive and reads as at odds with what *East Sussex County Council v TW* decided about EHCPs not to include wording to plan for potential change in circumstances: "*...a tribunal may not add information to Section I in order to avoid the risk of a placement breaking down.*"[83] Subsequent case law has reiterated this: "*...an Annual Review [of this EHC plan]...will provide the opportunity for the parties to decide on the...appropriate provision at that time and into the future.*"[84] Whilst EOTAS/C may not remain the appropriate provision for a child or young person, it has been established that an EHCP must simply address the here and now, i.e., the initial year-lifespan until an Annual Review is held and decision made.

Furthermore, if agreed that the local authority must at name a type of setting in Section I to satisfy Section 40(2) Children and Families Act 2014 then the local authority would have to agree not to consult with potential settings, given it would seem unnecessary. Whilst circumstances may mean a local authority does have to issue a final EHCP naming just a type of placement in Section I, such as ongoing consultations but agreement is already set on the type of setting, or to meet statutory deadlines in issuing a final EHCP including following an Annual Review. The local authority would be permitted to issue an amended final EHCP once a school or college was confirmed; the prior EHCP would remain legally viable until then.

The second option presented in *M & M v West Sussex County Council is* one that, whilst not a viable option for L, would gone on to be considered in greater detail in *NN v Cheshire East Council* and marked a significant

---

82 HS/2370/2017 Paragraph 68 (a) & (b) / [2018] UKUT 347 (AAC)

83 HS/1906/2016 Paragraph 32 / [2016] UKUT 0528 (AAC)

84 UA-2021-000606-HS Paragraph 12 / [2022] UKUT 230 (AAC) referring to "*...the tribunal's decision...in paragraph 8...*'

shift in how EOTAS/C is considered alongside a suitable school or college setting.

Beforehand, we must reconsider *Derbyshire County Council v EM and DM* (SEN)[85] which reaffirmed the decision in *M & M v West Sussex County Council* that Section I cannot name a child or young person's home. However, *Derbyshire* did not agree with the process to address Section I; Upper Tribunal Judge Wright confirmed:

> "*…if the local authority thinks that no school or other institution (or type of either) would be appropriate for the child, in my judgement the 'naming' duty under…sections 39(5) and 40(2) of the CFA…, and thus in section I of an EHC Plan, cannot as a matter of law arise.*"[86]

These sections of the Children and Families Act should be interpreted: "*…as a unified code*"[87] meaning:

> "*…section 61 makes the provision that sections 39(5) and 40(2) of the CFA deliberately leave out of account, namely the special educational provision that cannot be made appropriately in a school or other institution (or type of either).*"[88]

In applying such reasoning, there would be no requirement to name even a type of school of college in Section I, given that this would represent: "*…situations where sections 39(5) and 40(2) do not apply.*"[89] *Derbyshire* further examined the Regulations and legislation to confirm that the latter: "*…does not require a school or other institution (or type of either)*

---

85 HS/571/2019 & HS/572/2019 / [2019] UKUT 240 (AAC)

86 HS/571/2019 & HS/572/2019 Paragraph 15 / [2019] UKUT 240 (AAC)

87 HS/571/2019 & HS/572/2019 Paragraph 16 / [2019] UKUT 240 (AAC)

88 HS/571/2019 & HS/572/2019 Paragraph 16 / [2019] UKUT 240 (AAC)

89 HS/571/2019 & HS/572/2019 Paragraph 18 / [2019] UKUT 240 (AAC)

always to be named in section I of any EHC Plan."[90] This follows that the child or young person is not attending an institution, and so if they are: "*...to receive all...education by way of 'education otherwise than in school'...*"[91] thereby not meeting Regulation 12(1)(i) of the SEND Regulations and, secondly, section 37(2) not specifically stating that: "*...an EHC Plan is a plan naming the school or specifying the type of school that the child is to attend.*"[92]

Next is *NN v Cheshire East Council* (SEN)[93], with a vital judgement from the Upper Tribunal that examined *TM v London Borough of Hounslow, East Sussex County Council v TW* and *Derbyshire*, as well as summarising the legal processes for:

> "*...tribunals considering cases...where bespoke provision of education outside a conventional classroom setting end education otherwise than at school are proposed...*"[94]

Focusing on the proposals for W, the local authority requested Section I should name: "*...an Academy converter which...In addition to what may be described as typical special school provision, is also able to offer a varied school curriculum outside a conventional classroom setting.*"[95] Upper Tribunal Judge Rowley considered the options and legal processes to apply here, and found that:

> "*If...satisfied that the child will be present at a school or type of school for at least part of the time, that is sufficient and so the school or type of school must be specified in Section I. Attending provision provided*

---

90 HS/571/2019 & HS/572/2019 Paragraph 19 / [2019] UKUT 240 (AAC)

91 HS/571/2019 & HS/572/2019 Paragraph 20 / [2019] UKUT 240 (AAC)

92 HS/571/2019 & HS/572/2019 Paragraph 21 / [2019] UKUT 240 (AAC)

93 HS/260/2021 / [2021] UKUT 220 (AAC)

94 HS/260/2021 Paragraph 47 / [2021] UKUT 220 (AAC)

95 HS/260/2021 Paragraph 9 / [2021] UKUT 220 (AAC)

> *by the school as part of a bespoke package outside a conventional classroom setting will nonetheless mean that the school is to be attended by the chid within the meaning of regulation 12(1)(i).*"[96]

As previously established, it is only the school or college placement, and type, that can legally be named in Section I; for W, who was to receive bespoke provision through the named Academy: "*...it was not open to the tribunal to add anything to the name of school...the tribunal erred in law in the wording it chose to put in Section I, namely:*

> *Specialist Provision: [the school], Bespoke provision."*[97]

We will consider this judgement further in chapter eleven but, in summary, it is legally possible and practical to have EOTAS/C provision in Section F, plus a school or college named in Section I.

This leads us to a very recent decision, *JSH, R (On the Application OF) v Westmorland and Furness Council*[98] which concerned 'J', aged 17, who was "*...reliant on adults to meet the majority of his needs...due to his significantly reduced...functioning...*"[99] Following a breakdown in his previous specialist school placement, an EOTAS/C package was proposed for the upcoming autumn term. This was not in dispute in principle, but issue arose in trying to confirm an appropriate location to deliver this provision. J's previous school was considered as a temporary option but was dismissed:

> "*...based on sound and cogent reasons; J's peers had moved on; the school had confirmed that it could not meet his requirements; and there had been a few incidents which had given rise to staffing issues. In*

[96] HS/260/2021 Paragraph 47 f. / [2021] UKUT 220 (AAC)

[97] HS/260/2021 Paragraphs 54-55 / [2021] UKUT 220 (AAC)

[98] AC-2024-MAN-000345 / [2024] EWHC 3362 (Admin)

[99] Paragraph 5 AC-2024-MAN-000345 / [2024] EWHC 3362 (Admin)

short, a forced temporary period at UGS [the school] *was not in J's best interests.*"[100]

The local authority also proposed the EOTAS/C package to be delivered at J's home, again not a viable option due to immediate family circumstances and parental concerns that: "*...the proposed provider lacks adequate training.*"[101] Consideration was then given to:

"*...the option of locating EOTAS in the local area on an interim basis, but...was not pursued for a variety of reasons including incompatibility with existing Ofsted registration, difficulties with insurance cover or availability being limited.*"[102]

With few options, and the academic term already in progress:

"*The final preferred option...the setting up of a rented [Supported Living Home] SLH in Carlisle by CQC staff and with education provision to be provided within that home.*"[103]

was agreed as appropriate for J. Deputy High Court Judge Ridge appeared to take no issue with the location agreed (a care home) for J's EOTAS/C package to meet his special educational needs. Instead, the grounds of appeal focused on the local authority's delay in securing this residential setting and required adaptations so J could move there and so receive his EOTAS/C provision as per his EHCP. Interestingly, an example of the Section F provision included: "*A safe area close to his classroom...*"[104], which arguably should be amended given J was not to

---

[100] Paragraph 64 AC-2024-MAN-000345 / [2024] EWHC 3362 (Admin)

[101] Paragraph 31 AC-2024-MAN-000345 / [2024] EWHC 3362 (Admin)

[102] Paragraph 80 AC-2024-MAN-000345 / [2024] EWHC 3362 (Admin)

[103] Paragraph 81 AC-2024-MAN-000345 / [2024] EWHC 3362 (Admin)

[104] Paragraph 26 AC-2024-MAN-000345 / [2024] EWHC 3362 (Admin)

receive any of this provision within a school, even though a non-conventional classroom set-up.

A mandatory order was made confirming the timescales for the local authority to fully prepare the SLH for J to receive his EOTAS provision, noting that at the time there was:

> "*...nothing...in place for J's proposed EOTAS placement following his move to the property. There remain questions about the details and staffing of that package and matters still to be resolved and finalised.*"[105]

This is an interesting judgement that gives scope to, potentially, any type of setting (even if not classed as an educational institution, such as a care home) to be the location for Section F EOTAS/C provision. Arguably, J would be attending the setting (and staying there on a residential basis), but whether this would legally be classed as an educational institution, would be:

> "*...**a question of fact** for the specialist tribunal, taking account of all the **relevant evidence** including...those factors set out by Upper Tribunal Judge Lane in paragraph 33 of TB v Essex County Council (SEN) [2013] UKUT 0534 (AAC), namely: **regulation, governance, financing and administration.***"[106]

Importantly, at the time of writing, it is unknown what wording was included in Section I of J's EHCP, noting the time-limit on the mandatory order would have now expired, and all EOTAS/C provision in the supported living home should be in place. I, for one, will certainly be looking out for any further decisions that follow to see how broadly Section I can be interpreted when EOTAS/C is involved.

---

[105] Paragraph 87 AC-2024-MAN-000345 / [2024] EWHC 3362 (Admin)

[106] Paragraph 26 HS/260/2021 / [2021] UKUT 220 (AAC)

Our focus will now move to EOTAS/C and how this connects with personal budgets under Section J of an EHCP.

Section J – personal budget

Should EOTAC/S provision be included in Section F of an EHCP, then there is an option, although not an automatic right, for that provision to be funded through a personal budget as detailed in Section J:

> "*...This section should provide detailed information on any Personal Budget that will be used to secure provision in the EHC plan...*"[107]

Personal budgets are governed under Section 49 Children and Families Act 2014 and the Special Educational Needs (Personal Budgets) Regulations 2014, and are:

> "*...an amount of money identified by the local authority to deliver provision set out in an EHC plan where the parent or young person is involved in securing that provision...*"[108]

The methods for delivering personal budget are through direct payments to the child or young person's parents, an arrangement for the Section I placement (if there is one) to commission the provision, third party direct payments (such as to a child or young person's appointed Deputy under the Court of Protection), or a combination of these three.[109]

The local authority remains legally responsible for the Section F EOTAS/C provision through any of these methods, and it is worth noting that: "*Special educational provision acquired by means of a direct*

[107] Paragraph 9.69 SEND Code of Practice 2015

[108] Paragraph 9.95 SEND Code of Practice 2015

[109] Paragraph 9.101 SEND Code of Practice 2015

payment made by a local authority is to be treated as having been secured by the authority in pursuance of its duty under section 42(2)..."[110]

Requests for a personal budget from the child's parent, or young person themselves, can be put to the local authority when the EHCP is being drafted, at an Annual Review or if an EHC re-assessment is undertaken, with the assumption that the latter will lead to a revised EHCP being prepared.[111] Whilst local authorities have a duty to: "*...prepare a personal budget...if asked to do so by the child's parent or the young person*"[112] this duty requires consideration of the individual circumstances, and appears not to arise if preparing such a budget means: "...*the sum is part of a larger amount and disaggregation of the funds...:*

- *would have an adverse impact on services provided or arranged by the local authority for other EHC plan holders, or*
- *where it should not be an efficient use of the local authority's resources*"[113]

If either of these scenarios apply, then reasons must be provided to the child's parent, or young person, in writing and a right to request this decision is formally reviewed. Again, written reasons must be supplied following such a review.

Such "individual circumstances" may include if a child or young person's parents are already funding educational provision prior to EOTAS/C being agreed, and so directly employing the required professionals, such as tutors and therapists. If the provision being delivered is clearly detailed in Section F within EOTAS/C, then it would be reasonable to request a

---

110 Section 49(5) Children and Families Act 2014

111 Paragraph 9.98 SEND Code of Practice 2015

112 Section 49(1) Children and Families Act 2014

113 Paragraph 9.106 SEND Code of Practice 2015

personal budget to be set up through direct payments so the practical arrangement of these provisions could continue.

However, a local authority's agreement to a personal budget or EOTAS/C does not allow parental or a young person's choice of the professionals involved. EHCPs are not required, or expected, to name individuals, companies, or specific resources, for example. Discussions would need to be had with the local authority to confirm if existing experts could be retained to deliver the (now detailed) Section F EOTAS/C provision. Should the costs to do so be greater than an alternative provider, such as through the local authority or health board employment, who meets any training, qualification, or experience requirements set out in Section F, then the local authority would not be obliged to fund the additional costs; it would be anticipated that the parents would cover these. Alternatively, if agreement is not reached on the specific providers, then some parents may choose to self-fund those specific provisions, thus relieving the local authority of their duty to deliver that part of Section F. In such cases, consideration should be given to the benefits of removing the relevant wording from Section F thus ensuring that the local authority remains fully responsible for the entirety of the EHCP special educational provision and so meeting their Section 42(2) statutory duty.

CHAPTER SIX

WHAT EOTAS/C IS NOT

We have analysed the legal definition is of EOTAS/C and how this concept links into EHCPs, however it is also important to distinguish other situations when a child or young person may find themselves out of school or college. Understanding the legal and practical differences is necessary for advising clients and, crucially, confirming if the local authority maintains legal responsibility for the child or young person's education. As will be set out, there are key distinctions which can, nevertheless, be unclear in cases.

It is also important to discern if any of the following scenarios are altered if an EHCP is in place for that child or young person, as this can impact on the legal processes to adhere to.

a) Medically unfit to attend school or college

The first example is if a child or young person (of compulsory school age) is struggling to attend school or college at all, or full-time, because of a reason that has been diagnosed by a medical professional. A common example is due to anxiety, often over prolonged periods of time, or increasing in severity. Anxiety in relation to attending school or college can be exhibited through pupils being unable to leave their homes or the car at the start of the day, meaning the daily routine can become incredibly stressful for all those involved. Pupils may only be able to manage part of a day in attendance, or sometimes even less than this.

Establishing the reason for the child or young being unable to physically attend for the entirety of the set learning hours requires supporting evidence from a medical professional, usually a paediatrician or GP. Obtaining this specific type of evidence can be difficult; it must clearly address the cause for the absences and appropriately identify the medical reason for this. Sometimes families are faced with long waiting times to get this written evidence, or what they have been provided with is not as clear as it could be. Medical professionals may even be reluctant or unable to supply such evidence. In cases such as this:

> "*...the child's home school or the local authority should consider liaising with other medical practitioners and consider other evidence to ensure appropriate provision can be arranged as soon as possible.*"[114]

The aim of this to minimise delays and uncertainty to the pupil and their parents about the educational provision they will receive.

Securing sufficient medical evidence is essential, as this must be provided to both the local authority and school or college respectively. The former would need to accept this evidence and:

> "*...not demand continuing evidence without good reason, even where a child has long-term health problems.*"[115]

The local authority must confirm if the child or young person is officially marked as medically unfit to attend the placement in question.

Once confirmed, and it is understood that the child or young person will not be in attendance for a total of fifteen days, the local authority then has a legal duty to:

> "*... make arrangements for the provision of suitable. . . education at school or otherwise than at school for those children of compulsory*

[114] Page 8 Arranging education for children who cannot attend school because of health needs December 2023

[115] Page 8 Arranging education for children who cannot attend school because of health needs December 2023

> *school age who, by reason of illness...may not for any period receive suitable education unless such arrangements are made for them.*"[116]

To confirm, this legal duty also applies to pupils attending college provided they are of compulsory school age.

Subsequent guidance clarifies that a local authority must:

> "*...arrange suitable full-time education for children of compulsory school age who, because of physical or mental health illness, would not receive suitable education without such provision...*
>
> *The law does not define full-time education but children with health needs should have provision, where possible, which is equivalent to the education they would receive in a mainstream school.*"[117]

There may be situations when it would not be appropriate for full-time education to be in place, as:

> "*Alternative provision must be suitable to the child's age, ability and aptitude, and any special educational needs they have.*"[118]

The aim is for these pupils to not only maintain their education attainment and progression, but to also, if possible, return to a school or college setting. Ahead of any such return:

> "*Local authorities should work with schools to set up an individually tailored reintegration plan for each child: this could take the form of*

---

116 4 Section 19 Education Act 1996

117 Page 9 Arranging education for children who cannot attend school because of health needs December 2023

118 Page 8 Arranging education for children who cannot attend school because of health needs December 2023

> *an IHP* [Individual Healthcare Plan]. *This should need to include extra support to help fill any gaps arising from the child's absence.*"[119]

Parents do have recourse to legal action if the local authority is not providing alternative education, and the relevant evidence has been obtained and provided; as this duty on the legal authority is a legal one, formal methods of redress are available.

One option is for a formal complaint to be submitted to the local authority. Complaints must go through the respective local authority's stage one and two complaints processes. With the timescale usually up to twenty working days for the first stage alone to be exhausted, formal complaints are unlikely to be a viable option when, during this time, the pupil may remain without any, or sufficient, alternative educational provision in place from the local authority.

The other, arguably preferrable, option is to at least threaten the local authority with judicial review proceedings through a pre-action letter. Response timescales for a pre-action letter is fourteen days as standard. Often, such a letter can be sufficient to resolve the situation, especially when there is no outstanding medical evidence required, but of course the facts of each case would need to be considered to determine the most appropriate course of action.

In cases where a pupil is deemed medically unfit to attend school or college, they may or may not have an EHCP in place. If no, the EHCP process may have already been initiated, or at least considered. If an EHCP is maintained, then the local authority remains legally responsible to deliver the Section F provision if able to do so. Nevertheless, the local authority's Section 9 duty remains undiluted; suitable and appropriate alternative educational provision must be in place.

---

[119] Page 14 Arranging education for children who cannot attend school because of health needs December 2023

Being medically unfit to attend a school or college arguably provides the closest comparison to EOTAS/C given the reason for the absence is due to a child or young person's (medical) needs, and the local authority remains legally responsible for their educational provision. However, as set out in chapters four and five respectively, EOTAS/C focuses beyond a child or young person's SEN, and instead at what provision is specially required to meet those needs.

b) Elective home education

Under Section 42(5) Children and Families Act 2014 parents are legally entitled to make their own arrangements for their child's education e.g., teaching them at home. This means the child or young person needs to be off the school or college roll as necessary:

> "*Where a child or young person is a registered pupil and the parent decides to home educate, the parent must notify the school in writing that the child or young person is receiving education otherwise than at school and the school must then remove the pupil's name from the admission register... There is no provision in law for a 'trial period' of home education*".[120]

If the child or young person has an EHCP in place, then it is important to check the wording in Section I as, if reference is included that parents will be making their own educational arrangements, then this would relive the local authority of their legal duty to provide the Section F provisions at any named Section I placement, if there is one. Parents must therefore think very carefully before committing to this option. Whilst the EHCP would remain maintained by the local authority, its contents would essentially become academic and a simply point of reference for the child or young person's parents and any professionals involved.

---

[120] Paragraph 10.33 SEND Code of Practice 2015

The EHCP would continue to be reviewed at least annually, with part of this to consider if the Section F provisions remain necessary to meet the child or young person's special educational needs. This may be harder to determine if the provisions have not been fully delivered through elective home education; this is noting that parents are not legally required to deliver Section F provision, only:

> "*The parent of every child of compulsory school age shall cause him to receive efficient full-time education suitable -*
>
> *(a) to his age, ability and aptitude, and*
>
> *(b) to any special educational needs he may have, either by regular attendance at school or otherwise.*"[121]

Breaking down this definition in turn, firstly, "*efficient*":

> "*...can be interpreted as meaning education which 'achieves what it is intended to achieve'.*"[122]

For "*Full-time*", as noted earlier in this chapter:

> "*...the question of whether education for a specific child is full-time will depend on the facts of each case...*"[123]

Finally, there is "*suitable*":

121 Section 7 Education Act 1996

122 Page 7 Elective home education Departmental guidance for parents April 2019

123 Page 7 Elective home education Departmental guidance for parents April 2019

> *"...it must be age-appropriate, enable the child to make progress according to his or her particular level of ability, and should take account of any specific aptitudes..."*[124]

If, during elective home education, parents want to request the local authority meets its statutory duty to fund and deliver this provision i.e. through EOTAS/C, then they would need to gather evidence to put forward for an annual or interim review of the EHCP. Until any changes of wording to Section I are made and finalised, the child or young person's parents remain legally responsible for their education.

c) Exclusion

Finally, there are school or college exclusions. Any such exclusion must be lawful, proportionate and fair, with there being two types: fixed term/temporary and permanent.

Firstly, fixed term/temporary exclusion is when a pupil is temporarily removed from the school or college site due to disciplinary reasons. For the first five days following this, their school or college must provide and mark work set. Once the five days have passed, the setting must then arrange suitable full-time education. Forty-five days per year is the maximum that a pupil can be subject to a fixed term exclusion. During this time, the pupil remains on the school roll.

By contrast, a permanent exclusion is where a pupil is removed both from the school roll and the school itself. As per fixed term exclusions, full-time education needs to be in place after the fifth day, but here it is the local authority's responsibility to arrange. Parents have a right to request the exclusion goes through an independent review process; during this time, the pupil needs to remain on the Admissions Register.

---

[124] Page 7 Elective home education Departmental guidance for parents April 2019

Anything other than above i.e., an informal exclusion or part-time timetable is not following guidance and law. The latter may sometimes be required as, for example, part of a child's move to a new setting. Generally, pupils are entitled to receive a suitable full-time education i.e., not part-time, with the specific number of hours dependent on the pupil, including their age.

If a pupil has an EHCP, and is either temporarily or permanently excluded, then serious consideration must be given to the Section I named placement's suitability to meet that pupil's special educational needs in Section B and deliver the provision under Section F; it is very likely that an emergency or interim review of the EHCP would be required in such circumstances.

d) Summary of alternatives to EOTAS/C

This chapter highlights the potential range of scenarios when a child or young person may find themselves out of school or college. Complications and disputes as to who maintains legal responsibility for their education can arise from the outset, requiring clear evidence to distinguish if the reason is medically unfit, elective home education or an exclusion. In the first and third options, the local authority's legal duty to provide education remains, unless the pupil in question is subject to a fixed term exclusion.

We can now consider situations when a child or young person out of school or college does not meet any of the above criteria and, therefore, EOTAS/C is the viable legal option for them.

CHAPTER SEVEN

OUT OF SCHOOL – CONSIDERATIONS FOR WHEN EOTAS/C MAY BE REQUIRED

As we have identified in the previous chapters, there are legal requirements to meet before securing EOTAS/C in an EHCP. Let us now consider what practical factors may be relevant when assessing if EOTAS/C is appropriate; we do so based on none of the scenarios set out in chapter six being applicable.

For each prospective case regarding EOTAS/C, we must consider the following non-exhaustive list of criteria:

> *"...**all the circumstances** of the case in hand...:the **child's background** and **medical history**; the particular **educational needs** of the child; the **facilities that can be provided by a school**; the **facilities that could be provided other than in a school**; the comparative **cost** of the possible alternatives to the child's educational provisions; the **child's reaction to education provisions**, either at a school or elsewhere; the **parents' wishes**; and any other particular circumstances that apply to a particular child."*[125]

I have marked the key points in bold, in my opinion. *TM v London Borough of Hounslow* is clear that each case will depend on its own facts, thus allowing for potentially limitless submissions from both parents, or a young person, and respective local authorities. How much weight is applied to the various circumstances of each case will, again, depend on

125 Paragraph 26 *TM v London Borough of Hounslow* C1/2008/2712 / [2009] EWCA Civ 859, [2011] ELR 137

the individual situation. This also means that there is no automatic right to securing EOTAS/C if a child or young person presents with a similar profile of needs to another, and the latter has been deemed to required EOTAS/C.

There is also no requirement for both mainstream and specialist settings to have been tried prior to considering EOTAS/C as an appropriate option. Some children or young people may have been taught at home for prolonged periods of time, with the reasons for this contributing to the "*...circumstances of the case at hand...*"[126], whilst others may be in a placement that has broken down. This may be due to the sheer size and noise of the classroom/s, the way the lessons are taught, or having to navigate and respond to the ever-developing social rules and behaviours exhibited by their peers. Perhaps they are only able to attend the school or college for a limited time, if at all, and alternative placements may have also been considered and, or, consulted. We will go on to consider this point further in chapter eight.

It is useful to revisit *London Borough of Camden v KT*, where: "*...P had tried five schools unsuccessfully and there has been great difficulty in identifying suitable placement throughout these proceedings.*"[127]; compare this to the situation in *NN v Cheshire East Council* (SEN), where: "*W has never attended school.*"[128] There are also the contrasting decisions in *M v Hertfordshire County Council* and *AA & BB v Bristol City Council* both concerning school-based anxiety but the same conclusions were not reached about EOTAS/C being required.

As Section F provision can be wide-ranging, depending on the individual child or young person's needs, some may by their very nature be

---

126 Paragraph 26 *TM v London Borough of Hounslow* C1/2008/2712 / [2009] EWCA Civ 859, [2011] ELR 137

127 Paragraph 8 referring to paragraph 48 of the First-Tier Tribunal's judgement UA-2023-000056-HS / [2023] UKUT 225 (AAC)

128 Paragraph 4 HS/260/2021 / [2021] UKUT 220 (AAC)

inappropriate to be delivered in a school or college. An example is equine therapy, which must be undertaken at a stable, paddock, or menage through an official provider; such resources would not be found in an average maintained mainstream school.

Essentially, there can be varying circumstances to support EOTAS/C being the appropriate option for a child or young person; it is important to note that local authority 'blanket' policies cannot be relied on to determine these. Each case will depend on the evidence (this point will be considered in detail in chapter nine), as well as an assessment of what, if any, alternatives are being proposed. We will now go on to consider such alternatives in the next chapter.

CHAPTER EIGHT

WHY NOT TRY ANOTHER PLACEMENT?

A question that can be asked of parents when considering EOTAS/C is: "why not try another placement?"

As set out above, often multiple placements, of potentially varying types, may have been tried and tested without success. Sometimes there are physically no more options close enough to attend daily without significant complications, costs and to the detriment of the pupil in question. Furthermore, residential settings may not be what the child or young person has been identified to need nor an option wanting to be pursued. In situations like these, serious consideration must be given to available possibilities for that child or young person's education, and if this can be met in a school or college at all.

In some cases, schools or colleges that might have been previously disregarded may be reconsidered. Whether these are viable options to approach again, with the aim of securing a placement, depends on several factors as we shall now examine.

a) Types of placements except non-approved independent settings

First, it must be established what type of setting is being (re)considered. Placements are broadly divided into maintained, non-maintained and independent categories. We will consider one of the independent categories further on in this chapter, given there are different legal requirements to satisfy.

Let us look at the types of settings that, if requested to be named in Section I of an EHCP, must be consulted and named by the local authority:

- Local authority-maintained nursery school
- Local authority-maintained school/academy/free school (mainstream or special)
- Non-maintained special school
- Further education/sixth form college
- Independent school/independent specialist college which has been approved by the Secretary of State under Section 41 of the Children and Families Act 2014[129]

It is only if one, or both, of the following exceptions apply that a local authority does not have to name such a setting in Section I:

- *"It would be unsuitable for the age, ability, aptitude or SEN of the child or young person, or*
- *The attendance of the child or young person there would be incompatible with the efficient education of other, or the efficient use of resources"*[130]

As we will examine, there are further criteria dependant on the specific type of placement in question.

---

129 Paragraph 9.78 SEND Code of Practice 2015

130 Paragraph 9.79 SEND Code of Practice 2015; Section 39 (4) Children and Families Act 2014

b) Unable to meet needs

The first exception is if the placement would be unsuitable for the child or young person's SEN. Reasoning is required if a placement has concerns about meeting the Section B needs and being unable to deliver the Section F provision respectively. The local authority would still be able to overrule a setting, and name as the child or young person's Section I placement, even if such evidence was provided and the local authority was satisfied the setting could meet the needs with, for example, additional funding for staff employment, physical resources or therapeutic input.

There is a difference when considering maintained mainstream settings specifically. As pupils with SEN are entitled to be educated within this type of setting generally if that is their parental, or own (if a young person), preference,[131] this type of placement cannot cite unsuitability for refusing an offer of a place. Maintained mainstream schools and colleges can, potentially, rely on the second exception that is addressed in the following sub-section.

c) Attendance would impact on the other pupils' education

If the child or young person's attendance at the placement would be incompatible with the provision of efficient education of their peers whom they would be taught with, i.e., the pupils in the school or college who they would directly meet on a regular day-to-day basis.[132] This is the ground that schools or colleges may rely on when saying that they:

- Are over their Pupil Admission Number (PAN)

131 Section 33 (2) Children and Families Act 2014

132 Paragraph 9.79 SEND Code of Practice 2015

- Have no space in that particular year group

Settings saying they are full is insufficient; they have an active duty to evidence this incompatibility which, in practice, can be difficult to prove. Considering must be given to the other pupils': "*...age, ability, aptitude and any special educational needs they may have*"[133] and to show there are no reasonable steps possible to prevent this incompatibility. Should a maintained mainstream school or college successfully satisfy this requirement, then a local authority would not be obliged to name the placement in Section I of an EHCP.

It is important to note that standard school admissions criteria, including for secondary transition, do not apply when there is an EHCP in place and a potential school says they are full. The following criteria would be irrelevant in this instance:

- Suitability: Age, ability, aptitude or SEN. Note that the question of suitability for the child's SEN should have already been considered during the school consultation process.

- Children who are Looked After & Children who were Previously Looked After

- Siblings already attending (if criteria 1 is also satisfied)

- Faith: evidenced based on admissions requirements of the school (if criteria 1 is also satisfied)

- Distance order to home address, measured as a straight line (if criteria 1 is also satisfied)

[133] Paragraph 9.79 SEND Code of Practice 2015

d) The cost would exceed that of an alternative suitable setting, with the difference unjustified

This scenario concerns two placements, parental/young person preference and the local authority named setting, with the former being more costly to name in Section I and the benefits to the child or young person not outweighing the additional funds required. Often, but not always, parental or young person preference placement will be more expensive than the local authority's choice, meaning the question of suitability (to be considered ahead of costs) is essential.

e) Non-approved independent settings

There is another category of independent schools and specialist colleges. These are ones not approved by the Secretary of State under Section 41 of the Children and Families Act 2014. Parents can request one of these settings to be named in Section I, and the local authority must consider this request, but does not have a legal duty to consult with that setting.

Local authorities need to have regard to the general principle that children should be educated in accordance with their parents' wishes, unless:

> *"This would be incompatible with the efficient instruction and training, i.e. of the other pupils, or;*
>
> *The cost of placement would amount to unreasonable public expenditure, i.e. by comparing the total costs to the public purse, including transport, of both the parents' preferred placement versus the cost of the local authority's placement."*[134]

Even if none of the above exceptions apply, non-s41 settings do not have a duty to admit a child or young person even if named in Section I of an

---

[134] Section 9 Education Act 1996

EHCP. There is therefore an additional responsibility on the local authority to be satisfied that the setting would agree to the place before naming as the child or young person's placement. There are no options the parent, young person or local authority can take if such a setting does not agree to admission.

Furthermore, following the government's decision to add VAT onto independent school fees, if such a setting is named as the sole placement in Section I of a child or young person's EHCP, then there will be no VAT added onto the fees. Local authorities will continue to pay the fees and costs for all educational provision, the latter detailed in section F, unless alternative arrangements have been made.

If there are two schools named in Section I, and an independent placement is detailed as the parental preference, then the school fees and VAT will both remain the parents' responsibility to fund. This may happen when a local authority has named another placement as a school suitable for that child or young person's needs, which is not agreed to.

As a point of interest, the VAT addition is expected to be in force from 1 January 2025, with this also applying to any fees paid from 29 July 2024. The aim of the VAT is to fund public services, including education and maintained (state) schools.

CHAPTER NINE

WHAT IS NEEDED TO SUPPORT A REQUEST FOR EOTAS/C?

As an EOTAS/C request requires acceptance from the local authority that it would be inappropriate for a child or young person to receive special educational provision within a standard classroom set-up in an educational institution, having sufficient supporting evidence to meet this threshold is essential. We shall consider the different formats of such evidence, starting with professional experts and therapists.

a) Experts, including educational psychologists

Just as with any other requested amendments to an EHCP, relevant and clear evidence from appropriate professionals is required. This is unless existing evidence is sufficient, which will depend on the facts of each case. Note that local authority/health commissioned experts can, and may already, be involved in evidencing if a child or young person meets the legal definition to require EOTAS/C. However, given the arguably very high threshold to meet, careful consideration must be given as to how sufficient evidence will most likely be secured; from my experience, an independent expert is the advisable option.

Any evidence obtained needs to be from a suitably qualified expert, and one who is well-versed in not just the child or young person's needs, and the legalities and practicalities of EHCPs, but also in EOTAS/C if possible. A prime example of such an expert is an educational psychologist:

> "*Educational Psychologists (EPs)...work with children and young people usually between 0-25 years of age experiencing difficulties...to*

> *promote learning, develop emotional, social and behavioural skills and support psychological development.*"[135]

Educational psychologists, as per other therapists:

> "*…must have undergone appropriate training and achieved qualifications that are recognised by the Health and Care Professions Council (HCPC) as demonstrating…competence and "fitness to practise" as an educational psychologist.*"[136]

As with other professionals, educational psychologists often specialise in certain areas of special educational needs and disability. A review of their CV, website profile and/or any prior knowledge of their reports can usually clarify their suitability for the case at hand. Experts may also be able to recommend others if they themselves are unable to assist.

Formal assessments, unless this would not be in the child or young person's best interest, are recommended to provide as full a picture as possible for, primarily, the local authority. It needs to be clear what the child or young person's needs are and how these impact on their ability to access learning; this in turn will assist to clarify how, and where, provisions to meet these needs must be delivered.

London Borough of Camden v KT[137] gives an example of the importance of good educational psychologist evidence to support the inclusion of EOTAS/C provision in an EHCP. Here, the Tribunal accepted the parental submitted evidence for several reasons:

135 https://www.aep.org.uk/interested-career-educational-psychology - accessed 14.08.2024

136 https://www.aep.org.uk/interested-career-educational-psychology - accessed 14.08.2024

137 UA-2023-000056-HS / [2023] UKUT 225 (AAC)

> "*...Dr Kelly provided well-reasoned and clear answers to the questions...asked...His evidence was...more recent. Dr Kelly explained his conclusions with substantive reasons...*"[138]

What must also be remembered is that the Tribunal does not have to accept professional evidence in an EHCP appeal, even in the absence of contrary information as was the situation in this case:

> "*The law requires a tribunal to give adequate reasons for its conclusions. It was not obliged to accept Dr Kelly's evidence, despite the fact that it was expert evidence. It did not simply accept it; it explained why it did so ... That was adequate...*"[139]

Even though preference can be given to educational psychologists for gathering EOTAS/C evidence, that does not preclude other therapists from also doing so. Arguably, to provide as robust a case as possible, multiple expert reports may be needed. Examples could include speech and language therapists, occupational therapists and physiotherapists, as non-exhaustive examples:

> "*SLTs will work with children and young people (CYP) within the full range of educational settings...to support and enable CYP to reach their full communicative and educational potential and remove or reduce the barriers that their speech, language and communication needs (SLCN) present to their learning.*"[140]

> "*Occupational therapists can help children with a range of special needs. They usually evaluate an individual child's abilities and then recommend and provide them with special equipment or therapy...to*

---

138 Paragraph 21 referring to paragraphs 40&50 of the First-Tier Tribunal panel's decision UA-2023-000056-HS / [2023] UKUT 225 (AAC)

139 Paragraph 22 UA-2023-000056-HS / [2023] UKUT 225 (AAC)

140 https://www.rcslt.org/speech-and-language-therapy/where-slts-work/education/#section-1 – accessed 20.01.2025

> *help school-age children participate as fully as possible in educational activities...*"[141]

> "*Physiotherapists should be providing clear advice for all CYP who have additional physical needs impacting on their education. This should be in relation to access to the curriculum or in being able to participate in every day school life; in order to maximise function, participation and inclusion.*"[142]

As noted above, the key is any therapist focuses on areas within their expertise to address the child or young person's needs and provisions required. An example could be an occupational therapist commenting on school or college-sensory difficulties for the child or young person, and how a standard classroom setup exasperates these. This could be used to support special educational provision as being inappropriate to deliver in such an arrangement, and so advocating for EOTAS/C. Should an expert comment on, or recommend, provisions that could be held as outside of their professional remit, then there is a risk that a Tribunal could dismiss these, such as what happened in the First-tier Tribunal hearing in *M & M v West Sussex County Council (SEN)*:

> "*The views of the parents' OT about L's 'social, emotional and mental health' seem to have been rejected because she was considered to have expressed views on a matter failing outside of her professional approach.*"[143]

141 https://rcotss-ip.org.uk/what-is-occupational-therapy - accessed 20.01.2025

142 https://apcp.csp.org.uk/system/files/guidance_for_paediatric_physio therapists_writing_advice_for_education_health_and_care_plans.pdf – accessed 20.01.2025

143 Paragraph 27 HS/2370/2017 / [2018] UKUT 347 (AAC)

Another important point to remember is that even if the professional preparing the report is governed by the HCPC, or equivalent body:

> "*Health...provision which educates or trains a child or young person* ***must*** *be treated as special educational provision and included in Section F of the EHC plan. Decisions about whether health...provision should be treated as special educational provision* ***must*** *be made on an individual basis.*"[144]

Accompanying information to support EOTAS/C evidence should include the child or young person's personalised timetable for their current home education/requested EOTAS/C package. This will allow for greater detail on the timings and details of the provision that is not required in Section F; the latter must stick to the legal requirements, to set out what the provision is, frequency, duration and what type of professional will deliver this. Experts should be asked to advise on these points, rather than on such personalised specifics of the EOTAS/C package that potential changes in personnel or facilities could render these unenforceable under the EHCP. For example, if a named provider company closes, or an individual professional leaves that role; this is why such levels of detail are not expected or necessary in Section F of an EHCP.

As we will examine in chapter ten, appropriate expert evidence is required at any stage when EOTAS/C is being requested and, in anticipation of, being potentially rejected. What is initially relied on when requesting EOTAS/C includes the child's or young person's views; we shall now go on to examine the level of influence that these can have.

---

144 Paragraphs 9.73-9.74 SEND Code of Practice 2015

b) Child or young person's views

Section A of an EHCP must detail:

> *12.—(1) …*
>
> *(a) the views, interests and aspirations of the child…or the young person…*[145]

and so, as a starting point, such views must therefore be given appropriate weight, noting the individual's age, when considering the special educational provisions required for that child or young person.

The Upper Tribunal in *NN v Cheshire East Council (SEN)*[146] was required to consider if the First-tier Tribunal erred in law by not factoring in thirteen-year-old W's views when making the decision about his EOTAS/C provision and school placement respectively. This was considering the fact that:

> "*…both parties agreed that W's firm views should have been taking into account, or the tribunal should have explained why it considered they were not relevant.*"[147]

A key point of contention in *M & M v West Sussex County Council (SEN)*[148] was also that L's views about her educational provision and placement were not considered:

---

[145] Regulation 12(1) SEND Regulations 2014

[146] HS/260/2021 / [2021] UKUT 220 (AAC)

[147] Paragraph 50 HS/260/2021 / [2021] UKUT 220 (AAC)

[148] HS/2370/2017 / [2018] UKUT 347 (AAC)

> *"...despite the absence of an express...statutory requirement, the tribunal is required to consider a child's view's, wishes and feelings."*[149]

Here, Upper Tribunal Judge Mitchell held that the First-tier Tribunal had:

> *"...erred in law by failing to take into account L's views (see S v Worcestershire County Council [2017] UKUT 92 (AAC)). The EHC Plan, under the heading 'views, interests and aspirations'...reflected some of L's views but not...on an apparently central issue namely education at school...a letter...recorded L's view that she...was worried about being bullied and taken advantage of at school and wanted to be home-schooled for longer.*
>
> ...
>
> *...the tribunal was not required to make a decision in accordance with L's views but, since the merits of 'home-schooling', as compared with school attendance, was not addressed elsewhere in the tribunal's reasons, it was required to acknowledge her views and give an explanation...as to why it was making a decision that did not accord with her views."*[150]

Consideration must therefore be given to all relevant evidence, and not confined to the information recorded in Section A, which can often be out of date. Also, as Section A is not appealable to the SEND Tribunal, parties' attention can, naturally, focus on those Sections that can be formally challenged, such as Sections B, F and I respectively.

It is important that a child or young person's views are recorded in a manner that is appropriate and accessible for them, such as through video or audio clips, visual medium, or written statements, and the latter could

[149] Paragraph 1 HS/2370/2017 / [2018] UKUT 347 (AAC)

[150] Paragraphs 21 & 62 HS/2370/2017 / [2018] UKUT 347 (AAC)

even be provided by email if preferred. Furthermore, expert reports will usually include an account of their meeting with the child or young person, and their views or answers to questions or assessments put to them. These reports will also contain parental responses to points discussed, often containing background of the child or young person's educational and developmental progress.

Parental views on EHCP, including EOTAS/C provision, must also be considered along with other information, and we shall now look into this further.

c) Parental views

As one of the requirements on local authorities is to consult with parents when considering EOTAS/C,[151] the weight attributed to parental views needs to be understood. This is especially relevant as it is common for parents to initiate the request for EOTAS/C, and so having knowledge of how far this request can go is important when advising clients.

It is clear that: "*There is no statutory right for parents to request education otherwise than in a school.*"[152] Instead:

> "*...local authorities shall have regard to the general principle that pupils are to be educated in accordance with the wishes of their parents, so far as that is compatible with the provision of efficient instruction and training and the avoidance of unreasonable public expenditure.*"[153]

Therefore, having "*regard*" does not require local authorities to always agree to a parental request for EOTAS/C, as evidence may support this

[151] Section 61(2) Children and Families Act 2014

[152] HS/2370/2017 Paragraph 47 / [2018] UKUT 347 (AAC)

[153] Section 9 Education Act 1996

proposal, for example, as being too costly to justify (unreasonable public expenditure). Upper Tribunal Judge Rowley, when examining the Court of Appeal's decision in *TM v London Borough of Hounslow*[154] noted: "*...whilst Aikens LJ recognised the section 9 Education Act 1996 duty to have regard to parents' wishes, he emphasised that they cannot generally be determinative.*"[155]

As local authorities have no legal obligation to provide the best education for a child or young person through an EHCP, and only one that is appropriate and suitable, as noted in *R v Surrey CC ex p H*[156], focus must always remain on if EOTAS/C would meet, rather than exceed, this threshold compared to any placement or other educational alternatives. To determine if this threshold is met requires examination of not only the parents', child or young person's views, and any expert evidence, but also relevant information from the current, or previous placement, which we will now consider.

---

154 C1/2008/2712 / [2009] UKUT 240 (AAC)

155 *NN v Cheshire East County Council (SEN)* HS/260/2021 / [2021] UKUT 220 (AAC) referencing *TM v London Borough of Hounslow* C1/2008/2712 / [2009] UKUT 240 (AAC) paragraph 27: "***Consideration: parents' wishes...*** *That this exercise must include a consideration of the parents' wishes (under s 9 of the Act) is clear from the decision of Laws J, as he then was, in Catchpole v Buckinghamshire County Council and the Special Educational Needs Tribunal [1998] ELR 463, at 471F–472C. That statement was not questioned on appeal. The passages referred to were followed by Scott-Baker J, as he then was, in S and S v Bracknell Forest Borough Council and the Special Educational Needs Tribunal [1999] ELR 51, at 55. Those cases make clear that parental wishes cannot be determinative, except in the very rare case where there are otherwise equally balanced alternatives for the child's special educational needs.*"

156 (1984) 83 LGR 219

D) Current/previous placement views

It is useful to review any available, or potential, information from the child or young person's current, or previous school or college. Factors such as the pupil's attendance, progress, adjustments within class and to their timetable should all be considered. If a child or young person is struggling to attend their placement daily, and for the entire duration, then the reasons for this need to be examined to confirm if a 'conventional classroom set-up' is inappropriate; if so, then it would be reasonable to consider if EOTAS/C is a viable option. The placement's views will be essential in determining if the child or young person could still attend the setting through an EOTAS/C package; the provisions available and practical arrangements to make such attendance work would need to be confirmed and agreed upon.

Schools and colleges (aside from non-approved independent settings) will do well to remember that if they are named in Section I of a child or young person's final EHCP, then they must admit them. This would include situations where that pupil's attendance is not through a 'conventional classroom set-up'. Cooperating with the parents, young person local authority as required in determining the methods for delivering the EHCP provision will be crucial to reduce delays, disputes and potential detriment to the child or young person's educational progression (either in or outside of a placement).

CHAPTER TEN

IF EOTAS/C IS NOT AGREED, WHAT THEN?

As with any requested amendment/s to an EHCP, the decision initially lies with the responsible local authority; the other body with jurisdiction is the SEND Tribunal. We shall first examine the processes for directly querying a local authority decision about EOTAS/C.

a) Draft EHCP response

Following an EHC Needs Assessment, the local authority (if deemed required based on the provision the child or young person has been identified to need) will prepare a draft EHCP. This will bring together the evidence and information previously gathered (and listed under Section K as appendices). Section I must remain blank at the draft EHCP stage, with all other Sections to be competed as necessary.

The parents or young person will have at least fifteen days to consider the draft and submit a response, with this to include any content disagreed with and information requested to be added. There are various methods to do this, with some local authorities requiring a set response form to be completed. Often comments and requested changes are set out on the draft EHCP document itself (usually through WORD or sometimes a PDF, with the former being the more accessible option).

It is also open to use a process found in appeals to the SEND Tribunal called the Working Document. This provides the local authority and parents or young person with a set key for proposed changes to the draft EHCP content. Generally, local authority amendments are shown in italics, and with a strikethrough if asking to delete wording, and parents or a young person uses text in bold and with a strikethrough as needed. Proposed changes must be evidenced, for example through footnotes or comments, to promote an accessible document, with the aim for agreement to be reached by the time the EHCP is finalised. This may follow subsequent amended drafts and, or, meetings between the parties as required.

To try and expedite, or at least reduce any potential delays through this process, parents or the young person should already have secured their evidence supporting the EOTAS/C provision being requested. This may have been sourced through the EHC Needs Assessment stage through local authority instructed professionals or, more likely, through independent reports as discussed in chapter nine. Should parents or the young person wish to gather such evidence once the EHCP has been drafted, then there is the risk of the local authority not agreeing to the extra time and so the EHCP being finalised without a full parental or young person response. This is noting that the statutory timeframe from requesting an EHC Needs Assessment to issue a final EHCP (excluding any appeals to the SEND Tribunal) is twenty weeks.[157] However, cases can, and do, exceed this timeframe for various reasons; this may allow parents or the young person further opportunity to try and agree the EOTAS/C provision the local authority ahead of the final EHCP being issued.

Once this has happened, there will be additional stages when disputes over EOTAS/C provision can be addressed, which we will now go on to consider.

[157] Regulation 13(2) SEND Regulations 2014

b) Annual Review

One scenario is that a request for EOTAS/C has been put forward for an Annual Review of the EHCP and done so at least two weeks prior to the scheduled date.[158] This request should include evidence to support the legal threshold having been met (as discussed in chapter four), plus relevant and recent expert evidence (as discussed in chapters seven and nine respectively).

During the Review, the written request and evidence can be elaborated and expanded upon as necessary, whilst also seeking confirmation of the views of the other attendees.[159] To strengthen the request, it is advisable to gather prior support from those attendees in writing, which can then be reaffirmed during the Review.

Within two weeks of the Review, either the local authority (if the child or young person is not attending an educational placement) or the school or college must prepare written recommendations, following the evidence submitted.[160] Within a further two weeks, so four weeks maximum from the Review, the local authority must issue its decision if the EHCP will remain as is, be amended (and set out these proposed changes) or be ceased. The parents or young person will have a right of appeal to the SEND Tribunal on receipt of the first or third decision.[161] Once a response has been provided to the proposed EHCP changes from the local authority, a final EHCP will be issued, then enabling a right of appeal. If the scope of amendments does not sufficiently detail the EOTAS/C provision sought after, then the next option is to request

---

[158] Regulations 20 & 21 (2) SEND Regulations 2014

[159] Regulations 20 & 21 (2) SEND Regulations 2014

[160] Regulations 20 (7), (8), (9) & 21 (7), (8) SEND Regulations 2014

[161] Regulations 20 (10), (11) & 21 (9), (10) SEND Regulations 2014

mediation with the local authority, ahead of appealing, to the SEND Tribunal, which we shall now examine.

c) Mediation

Mediation can be requested if a parent or young person disagrees with Sections B, F, either with without Section I, of a final EHCP; a sole dispute concerning Section I does not require a mediation certificate.[162] Whilst this does not prevent a parent or young person asking for mediation to address a Section I dispute, in my experience local authorities can be reluctant to engage and often referring to (usually) a previous panel decision having been made and remaining unchanged without an appeal to the SEND Tribunal.

For a request for EOTAS/C provision, it is likely all three Sections, so Sections B (to confirm the needs requiring EOTAS/C is sufficient), Section F (to ensure the actual provisions cover all of those needs) and potentially Section I (to name a school or college should some of the EOTAS/C provision be planned to take place here) will need to be challenged. The case may be that Section I names a school or college when in fact the EOTAS/C provision is not to be delivered through this setting; here, Section I would need to be amended to be blank for both name and type of placement.

Otherwise, a local authority must arrange mediation within thirty days of a request[163] and ensure they attend and participate (to include making decisions), as well as confirming that the mediator is independent.[164] However, should a local authority not complete these steps, then the mediation provider will issue the parents or young person with a

162 Sections 52, 54, 55 Children and Families Act 2014 & Regulation 32, 33, 36(1) SEND Regulations 2014

163 Regulation 36(2) SEND Regulations 2014

164 Section 54(2) Children and Families Act 2014 &

mediation certificate, allowing them a further month in which to appeal. This will have followed the initial two months to contact mediation from the date of the local authority's decision letter that must accompany the final EHCP.

Mediation can be an appropriate option if there is new evidence, not previously available for the Review or when the EHCP was being drafted and finalised. Putting forward such evidence would need to happen ahead of the scheduled mediation date, and relevant parties confirmed to attend. These can include legal representation, should the parents or young person request this.[165] At the conclusion of the mediation, the parties will review and sign a mediation agreement, which will be legally enforceable and confirm the timings for the next steps each party will take. Provided such steps resolve the dispute that the parent or young person was initially challenging, such as the content of any EOTAS/C provision in Section F, or that fact that there was no such content, then an appeal to the SEND Tribunal will not be required, certainly at that stage of the EHCP timeline.

From my experience, it is worth considering the practical implications of requesting and partaking in mediation ahead of any subsequent appeal.

Local authorities are required to arrange mediation within thirty days of receiving notice of this request. Mediation can still take place even after this timeframe has passed, and there appears to be little recourse if a local authority does not arrange the mediation at all. These potential delays should be factored into the overall timings of an appeal, if required, as well as considering the need for any additional evidence as the matter progresses. These points will be further examined in the next part of this chapter.

Going back to mediation, whilst it is required that local authority representatives who attend can agree on decisions there and then, some

---

165 *L Kumar v LB of Hillingdon* [2020] EWHC 3326 (Admin)

report that they need to submit the parental or young person's position to a separate panel decision beforehand. This can mean matters progress very little during the actual mediation, and the options and timings following this will depend on the terms of the mediation agreement signed by both parties. Practically, there are limited options should you find yourself in mediation with a local authority representative who is unable to make decisions at that stage without additional panel confirmation. Ultimately, it is the mediator's role to ensure all parties who agree to attend are willing and able to decide on matters there and then; this is something that should be set before the mediation date.

Should mediation not provide a resolution to the disputes in Sections B, F and potentially I, then the next option available to the parent or young person is to submit an appeal to the SEND Tribunal.

d) Appeal to the SEND Tribunal

The First-tier Tribunal (SEND) is: "*...responsible for handling appeals against local authority decisions regarding special educational needs, including a refusal to:...change the sections of an existing EHC plan which are about education (sections B, F and I).*[166] The SEND Tribunal is under the remit of the Health, Education and Social Care Chamber within the First-tier Tribunal system.[167]

There are prerequisite forms and information that must be completed and supplied to successfully submit an appeal. This includes the:

[166] https://www.gov.uk/courts-tribunals/first-tier-tribunal-special-educational-needs-and-disability & https://www.gov.uk/appeal-ehc-plan-decision – accessed 12.01.2025

[167] https://www.gov.uk/courts-tribunals/first-tier-tribunal-special-educational-needs-and-disability – accessed 12.01.2025

- Final EHCP
- Section K appendices
- Local authority's decision letter that must accompanying the above
- Mediation certificate
- SEND35 form

In addition, available supporting evidence needs to be provided, such as expert reports not included in the Section K appendices, but which are recent and relevant to the EOTAS/C provision being requested.

Appeal timetables are currently taking approximately eight-fourteen months from being registered to a final hearing date, and so forward planning as to further evidence and any potential updates to EOTAS/C provision being sought will be necessary. Both parties will be allowed opportunity to submit additional evidence, usually around twelve weeks from the date of the appeal being registered. Based on the current timetables, this this leaves several months until the scheduled hearing date, and so aiming to resolve the appeal through negotiations with the local authority is often advisable.

The viability of such negotiations will usually be clear, or certainly clearer, once the local authority response deadline to the appeal has passed. This is usually set for six weeks from the date of registration. The Tribunal encourages parties to work together on addressing the content of the EHCP disputes, through the Working Document process previously referred to. Any issues not resolved by the hearing date will require the Tribunal's consideration and decision. Types of hearings vary between in-person, albeit remote in most cases, on the papers, or a hybrid hearing. A request is required for a paper, in person or hybrid hearing, and opportunities arise through the course of an appeal to confirm if any of these are applicable; the Tribunal would have to agree to any such requests, factoring in the local authority response as well.

Appeals allow for both parties to gather up to date, or new, evidence. This can require planning around timings to ensure that any formal standardised assessments are not duplicated between separately instructed experts. Findings also need to be shared, and experts encouraged to discuss these with their contemporaries. Should issues arise around potential over assessment or in complying with such requests, then the Tribunal can be asked to intervene and issue an Order to confirm what is required from either/both parties.

Evidence in respect of EOTAS/C will need to include an assessment of the child or young person within their current educational set-up, as well as experts visiting, or at least reviewing from the relevant papers, the school or college, if there is one, being proposed to deliver some of this provision. If the child or young person is already attending that setting, then as assessment at that venue as well as in the other location/s they already receive or are proposing to receive, EOTAS/C provision will be necessary. Experts are also encouraged to speak with professionals already involved in supporting the child or young person, as well as the parents as standard.

Should a local authority be proposing a placement, which the parents or young person do not agree is suitable or appropriate to deliver part of the EOTAS/C provision, then evidence from the latter will need to focus on knocking out this placement, as well as satisfy the legal requirement that it would be inappropriate for any school or college to deliver such provision through a conventional classroom set-up.

If EOTAS/C provision is agreed or ordered in Section F, and potentially a Section I placement named to deliver some of these provisions through a non-conventional classroom set-up, then the local authority will be legally responsible for delivering this in full. The timings of when this responsibility starts will depend on when agreement, or an order, is set.

The maximum timeframe expected is five weeks plus one day from the date of a final Tribunal order.[168]

If EOTAS/C is not ordered to be included in an EHCP, parents or a young person can only challenge this decision of the First-tier Tribunal if there has been:

- an error in law, or
- additional information or evidence that would need to be considered has become available since the appeal hearing

and neither situation is common. Legal advice should be sought if considering appealing to the Upper Tribunal in either circumstance, noting the strict time, as well as legal, requirements for successfully doing so.[169]

[168] https://www.gov.uk/government/publications/time-limits-for-complying-with-a-send-tribunal-decision-send18/carry-out-an-order-in-special-educational-needs-cases – accessed 29.01.2025

[169] https://www.gov.uk/administrative-appeals-tribunal/how-to-appeal – accessed 29.01.2025

CHAPTER ELEVEN

A FLEXIBLE TAKE ON EOTAS/C – A SIGN OF PROGRESS, OR CAUSE FOR AMBIGUITY?

As we have seen in chapter four, the legal definition of EOTAS/C has not remained consistent through progression from the Education Act 1996 to the Children and Families Act 2014. A reminder of both is useful here:

> *(1) Where a local authority are satisfied that it would be* *inappropriate* (emphasis added) *for-*
>
> *(a) the special educational provision which a learning difficulty of a child in their area calls for, or*
>
> *(b) any part of such provision,*
>
> *to be made in a school, they may arrange for the provision (or, as the case may be, for part of it) to be made otherwise than in a school.*[170]
>
> (1) *A local authority in England may arrange for any special educational provision that it has decided is necessary for a child or young person for whom it is responsible to be*
>
> *made otherwise than in a school….*

[170] Section 319 Education Act 1996

> (2) *An authority may do so only if satisfied that it would be* *inappropriate* (emphasis added) *for the provision to be made in a school...*[171]

The key difference is the wording "*any part of*" compared with "*any*"; the former reads as if all the special educational provision requiring EOTAS/C is one combined entity, with sub-sections of this open to be made in a school (or college), and the latter suggesting that EOTAS/C provision is divided into individual entries set out in Section F, and so requiring confirmation if each one would be inappropriate to be made in a school (or college). The specifics of the wording were considered by Upper Tribunal Judge Mitchell:

> "*Section 61(1) conferred power on a local authority to arrange for "any special educational provision" that is has decided is necessary to be made otherwise than in a school, rather than "the special educational provision".*[172]

Upper Tribunal Judge Rowley examined the addition of "*necessary*" in Section 61, concluding that "*inappropriate*" is the essential definition across both Acts.[173] He also noted:

> "*...section 319 specifically permits a local authority to arrange for any part of special educational provision to be made otherwise than in a school. There is no such explicit empowerment in section 61. Nonetheless...there is nothing to suggest that such a power should not*

[171] Section 61 Children and Families Act 2014

[172] *M & M v West Sussex County Council (SEN)* Paragraph 68 (b) HS/2370/2017 / [2018] UKUT 347 (AAC)

[173] *NN v Cheshire East County Council (SEN)* Paragraph 31 HS/260/2021 / [2021] UKUT 220 (AAC)

> *be inferred in section 61 and…the reference to 'any' in section 61(1) implies that the power does still exist.*"[174]

Arguably, both definitions could therefore support a local authority, or parent or young person, submitting that not all EOTAS/C provision must be delivered outside of a school or college. How far such submissions go would depend on the individual facts and, if in an appeal, how the SEND Tribunal judge and panel interpret the legislation. This would then affect how the provision is to be detailed, and enforced, through the EHCP.

An interesting example is also in *M & M v West Sussex County Council (SEN)*[175], where consideration was given to the absolute requirement for a placement, or type to be named in Section I[176], when EOTAS/C was to be detailed in Section F. One option was presented as:

> "*…an educational package involving elements of attendance at a school and otherwise than in a school…section 61 provision and school attendance are not necessarily mutually exclusive.*"[177]

This leads us back to the "*summary and guidance*" from Upper Tribunal Judge Rowley for:

[174] *NN v Cheshire East County Council (SEN)* Paragraph 30 HS/260/2021 / [2021] UKUT 220 (AAC) – note that "*part*" is italicised in the decision

[175] HS/2370/2017 / [2018] UKUT 347 (AAC)

[176] Sections 39-40 Children and Families Act 2014

[177] Paragraph 68 (b) HS/2370/2017 / [2018] UKUT 347 (AAC)

> "*…cases…where bespoke provision of education outside of a conventional classroom setting and education otherwise than at school are proposed…*"[178]

On considering the special educational provisions put forward, clarification was given as follows:

> "*…if…it would be inappropriate for any…to be made in any school, then Section I must*
>
> *be left blank...*
>
> *…if the tribunal is not satisfied that it would be inappropriate…it follows that a particular school or type of school would be appropriate for the child…in relation to at least part of the provision…*"[179]

The decision went on to set out a significant shift in the link between EOTAS/C and Section I:

> "*…the tribunal must consider whether the school or type of school will be 'attended by' the child. If it is satisfied that the child will be present at a school or type of school for at least part of the time…as part of a bespoke package outside of a conventional classroom setting…that is sufficient and so the school or type…must be specified in Section I.*"[180]

This judgement gave scope for EOTAS/C provision to become more personalised and move beyond any pre-existing notion that no school or college could be involved when EOTAS/C was in place. For some

---

[178] *NN v Cheshire East County Council (SEN)* Paragraph 47 HS/260/2021 / [2021] UKUT 220 (AAC)

[179] *NN v Cheshire East County Council (SEN)* Paragraph 47 c & d HS/260/2021 / [2021] UKUT 220 (AAC)

[180] *NN v Cheshire East County Council (SEN)* Paragraph 47 f HS/260/2021 / [2021] UKUT 220 (AAC)

children and young people, continuing to access provision through their previous, or a new placement, may be appropriate for their needs. This could include receiving hydrotherapy in the school or college pool, attending social skills groups, or music therapy within an established music provision. These are examples only, and each situation involving EOTAS/C will be different and require relevant professional evidence, as discussed in chapter nine.

If a current or previous placement is supportive of the proposed EOTAS/C provisions, and the parents or young person agrees then that placement would need to be named as Section I placement by the local authority or Tribunal, if satisfied by the evidence submitted. That placement would legally have to admit that child or young person, once the EHCP is finalised, provided there are no caveats, or the school or college is solely independent (non-approved) and not offered a place. Clarification would also need to be included in Section F for the EOTAS/C provision to be delivered outside of the placement, with the remaining to be legally met by the setting, as with any other EHCP where a school or college is named. The local authority would also still be legally responsible for all of Section F, including provisions covered through EOTAS/C, and the child or young person's attendance (even if through a bespoke package outside of a conventional classroom setting) at the named Section I placement.

Naturally, even personalised school or college attendance will not be appropriate for every child or young person, which the Upper Tribunal has acknowledged: "*…the 2014 Regulations…anticipate that some children with an EHC Plan might not be receiving education in a school.*"[181] The very terminology of Education Otherwise Than At School or College does not promote pupils attending either type of setting; some may find the idea of incorporating a placement into an EOTAS/C package contradictory. This would be a reasonable view, especially if a previous placement, or more than one, have broken down. It also poses

[181] Paragraph 69 HS/2370/2017 / [2018] UKUT 347 (AAC)

the question of why the legislation does not specifically account for EOTAS/C provision to include some form of attendance at a school or college if appropriate. Perhaps such clarifications will be proposed in time; until then, the lack of tailored guidance in the legislation and regulations will remain open to interpretation from both parents, and young people, and local authorities.

This thought leads us to the final chapter of this guide, moving on from EOTAS/C.

CHAPTER TWELVE

EOTAS/C – WHAT IS NEXT?

We have examined the history of EOTAS/C through the Education Act 1996 to the implementation of the Children and Families Act 2014, and the ten years following this. What case law has shown us is that the interpretation of, and addressing gaps in, legislation has enabled varying decisions and challenges on how and when EOTAS/C can be applicable. EOTAS/C has gone from:

- all provision to be delivered outside of a school or college, to
- attending such a placement but not through a standard classroom set-up, to
- potentially being at a residential supported living home.

The flexibility, or ambiguity, of the progression of EOTAS/C case law, within a relatively short period of time, supports the indivdual needs of children and young people as being a central aspect to any EOTAS/C request to a local authority, or appeal to the SEND Tribunal. Arguments can be made on both sides, and so clear and relevant professional evidence will be needed to fully support each position.

Consideration about if it remains inappropriate for a child or young person to attend a setting through a standard classroom set-up should usually need to be discussed prior to, and at, an Annual Review of an EHCP. The EOTAS/C provision could remain, proposed changes set out or to have this removed entirely. Arguably, some parents who seek EOTAS/C for their child do not do so with a view that they will never attend a school or college again. Sometimes EOTAS/C is a necessary stopgap between school or college placements, whether this was the original intention or not. Ultimately, each case must turn on its own merits and so consider:

> "*Without being an exhaustive list…:*
>
> *i. the child's background and medical history;*
>
> *ii. the particular educational needs of the child;*
>
> *iii. the facilities that can be provided by a school;*
>
> *iv. the facilities that could be provided other than in a school;*
>
> *v. the comparative cost of the possible alternatives to the child's educational provisions, either at school or elsewhere;*
>
> *vi. the parents' wishes (although they are not generally determinative); and*
>
> *vii. any other particular circumstances that apply to a particular child…*"[182]

It will be interesting to see if there is an increase in parental requests for EOTAS/C, particularly following the extended periods during the national COVID-19 lockdowns in 2020-2021 when many children and young people with EHCPs were educated through bespoke means, and, or, out of school or college entirely.

Ultimately, serious thought and commitment needs to be shown if seeking EOTAS/C but, sometimes, it is the only solution. How soon that is decided, or agreed upon, will depend on the evidence, local authority, and the child and young person at the centre of it all. As at any stage of the EHCP process:

---

182 Paragraph 47 b) HS/260/2021 / [2021] UKUT 220 (AAC)

> *...a local authority in England must have regard to the following matters in particular—*
>
> *(a) the views, wishes and feelings of the child and his or her parent, or the young person...*[183]

Hopefully, those views on EOTAS/C are given due regard and, crucially, acted upon in a timely manner so children and young people with EHCPs will receive an education that meets all their special educational needs, in whatever form they require, and so: "*...achieve the best possible educational...outcomes.*"[184] I, for one, will be curious to see what happens next in the ever-changing legal world of EOTAS/C.

183 Section 19 (a) CFA 2014

184 Section 19 (d) CFA 2014

MORE BOOKS BY LAW BRIEF PUBLISHING

A selection of our other titles available now:-

'A Practical Guide to Probation Breaches and Other Applications' by Mark Thomas
'A Practical Guide to Remarriage and Divorce' by Cordelia Williams & Claire Howard
'A Practical Guide to Privacy, Transparency, Reporting Restrictions and Closed Proceedings in the Court of Protection' by Laura Mannering
'Beaumont on Barristers – A Guide to Defending Disciplinary Proceedings (Second Edition)' by Marc Beaumont
'A Practical Guide to Payments for Environmental Services' by Ben Sharples
'A Practical Guide to the Law of Pregnancy and Maternity at Work' by Rebecca Thomas
'A Practical Guide to Redundancy – Second Edition' by Philip Hyland & Collette Moore
'A Practical Guide to International Issues for Scottish Family Lawyers' by Susie Mountain, Donna McKay, Ken MacDonald
'A Practical Guide to the Law on Deprivation of Liberty' by Ben Troke
'A Practical Guide to Rights over Airspace and Subsoil – Second Edition' by Daniel Gatty
'A Practical Guide to the Law in Relation to Inquests' by Ramya Nagesh
'A Practical Guide to the Construction and Rectification of Wills and Trust Instruments (Second Edition)' by Edward Hewitt
'A Practical Guide to Data Protection in Social Housing' by Clare Paterson
'A Practical Guide to Spousal Maintenance – Second Edition' by Liz Cowell
'A Practical Guide to International Parental Child Abduction Law (England and Wales)' by Dr Onyója Momoh
'A Practical Guide to Deprivation of British Citizenship' by Sean Ell
'A Practical Guide to Commercial Property Service Charges' by Rachel Garton
'A Practical Guide to Clinical Negligence – Third Edition' by Geoffrey Simpson-Scott (Geoff)
'A Practical Guide to the Rights of Grandparents in Children Proceedings – Second Edition' by Stuart Barlow

'The Electronic Communications Code: A Practical Guide – Second Edition' by Kerry Bretherton KC, James Castle, Mark Loveday

'A Practical Guide to the Independent School Standards – September 2023 Edition' by Sarah McKimm

'A Practical Guide to Estate Administration and Crypto Assets' by Richard Marshall

'A Practical Guide to Parental Alienation in Private and Public Law Children Cases' by Sam King QC & Frankie Shama

'Contested Heritage – Removing Art from Land and Historic Buildings' by Richard Harwood QC, Catherine Dobson, David Sawtell

'The Limits of Separate Legal Personality: When Those Running a Company Can Be Held Personally Liable for Losses Caused to Third Parties Outside of the Company' by Dr Mike Wilkinson

'A Practical Guide to Transgender Law' by Robin Moira White & Nicola Newbegin

'A Practical Guide to 'Stranded Spouses' in Family Law' by Mani Singh Basi

'A Practical Guide to Residential Freehold Conveyancing' by Lorraine Richardson

'A Practical Guide to Pensions on Divorce for Lawyers' by Bryan Scant

'A Practical Guide to Challenging Sham Marriage Allegations in Immigration Law' by Priya Solanki

'A Practical Guide to Digital Communications Evidence in Criminal Law' by Sam Willis

'A Practical Guide to Legal Rights in Scotland' by Sarah-Jane Macdonald

'A Practical Guide to New Build Conveyancing' by Paul Sams & Rebecca East

'A Practical Guide to Inherited Wealth on Divorce' by Hayley Trim

'A Practical Guide to Practice Direction 12J and Domestic Abuse in Private Law Children Proceedings' by Rebecca Cross & Malvika Jaganmohan

'A Practical Guide to Confiscation and Restraint' by Narita Bahra QC, John Carl Townsend, David Winch

'A Practical Guide to the Law of Forests in Scotland' by Philip Buchan

'A Practical Guide to Health and Medical Cases in Immigration Law' by Rebecca Chapman & Miranda Butler

'A Practical Guide to Bad Character Evidence for Criminal Practitioners by Aparna Rao

'A Practical Guide to Extradition Law post-Brexit' by Myles Grandison et al

'A Practical Guide to Hoarding and Mental Health for Housing Lawyers' by Rachel Coyle

'Stephens on Contractual Indemnities' by Richard Stephens
'A Practical Guide to the EU Succession Regulation' by Richard Frimston
'A Practical Guide to Solicitor and Client Costs – Second Edition' by Robin Dunne
'Constructive Dismissal – Practice Pointers and Principles' by Benjimin Burgher
'A Practical Guide to Religion and Belief Discrimination Claims in the Workplace' by Kashif Ali
'A Practical Guide to the Law of Medical Treatment Decisions' by Ben Troke
'Fundamental Dishonesty and QOCS in Personal Injury Proceedings: Law and Practice' by Jake Rowley
'A Practical Guide to the Law in Relation to School Exclusions' by Charlotte Hadfield & Alice de Coverley
'A Practical Guide to Divorce for the Silver Separators' by Karin Walker
'The Right to be Forgotten – The Law and Practical Issues' by Melissa Stock
'A Practical Guide to Planning Law and Rights of Way in National Parks, the Broads and AONBs' by James Maurici QC, James Neill et al
'A Practical Guide to Election Law' by Tom Tabori
'A Practical Guide to the Law in Relation to Surrogacy' by Andrew Powell
'A Practical Guide to Claims Arising from Fatal Accidents – Second Edition' by James Patience
'A Practical Guide to Asbestos Claims' by Jonathan Owen & Gareth McAloon
'A Practical Guide to Stamp Duty Land Tax in England and Northern Ireland' by Suzanne O'Hara
'A Practical Guide to the Law of Farming Partnerships' by Philip Whitcomb
'A Practical Guide to the Law of Unlawful Eviction and Harassment – Second Edition' by Stephanie Lovegrove
'A Practical Guide to Costs in Personal Injury Claims – Second Edition' by Matthew Hoe
'A Practical Guide to the General Data Protection Regulation (GDPR) – Second Edition' by Keith Markham
'A Practical Guide to Working with Litigants in Person and McKenzie Friends in Family Cases' by Stuart Barlow
'Protecting Unregistered Brands: A Practical Guide to the Law of Passing Off' by Lorna Brazell
'A Practical Guide to Secondary Liability and Joint Enterprise Post-Jogee' by Joanne Cecil & James Mehigan

'A Practical Guide to the Pre-Action RTA Claims Protocol for Personal Injury Lawyers' by Antonia Ford
'A Practical Guide to Neighbour Disputes and the Law' by Alexander Walsh
'A Practical Guide to Coercive Control for Legal Practitioners and Victims' by Rachel Horman
'A Practical Guide to the Law of Driverless Cars – Second Edition'
by Alex Glassbrook, Emma Northey & Scarlett Milligan
'A Practical Guide to TOLATA Claims' by Greg Williams
'A Practical Guide to Elderly Law – Second Edition' by Justin Patten
'A Practical Guide to Responding to Housing Disrepair and Unfitness Claims' by Iain Wightwick
'A Practical Guide to the Law of Bullying and Harassment in the Workplace' by Philip Hyland
'How to Be a Freelance Solicitor: A Practical Guide to the SRA-Regulated Freelance Solicitor Model' by Paul Bennett
'A Practical Guide to Prison Injury Claims' by Malcolm Johnson
'A Practical Guide to Advising Clients at the Police Station' by Colin Stephen McKeown-Beaumont
'A Practical Guide to Antisocial Behaviour Injunctions – Second Edition' by Iain Wightwick
'Practical Mediation: A Guide for Mediators, Advocates, Advisers, Lawyers, and Students in Civil, Commercial, Business, Property, Workplace, and Employment Cases' by Jonathan Dingle with John Sephton
'The Mini-Pupillage Workbook' by David Boyle
'A Practical Guide to Crofting Law' by Brian Inkster
'A Practical Guide to the Law of Domain Names and Cybersquatting' by Andrew Clemson
'A Practical Guide to the Law of Gender Pay Gap Reporting' by Harini Iyengar
'NHS Whistleblowing and the Law' by Joseph England
'Employment Law and the Gig Economy' by Nigel Mackay & Annie Powell
'A Practical Guide to Noise Induced Hearing Loss (NIHL) Claims' by Andrew Mckie, Ian Skeate, Gareth McAloon
'An Introduction to Beauty Negligence Claims – A Practical Guide for the Personal Injury Practitioner' by Greg Almond
'Intercompany Agreements for Transfer Pricing Compliance' by Paul Sutton
'Zen and the Art of Mediation' by Martin Plowman
'A Practical Guide to Adoption for Family Lawyers' by Graham Pegg

www.ingramcontent.com/pod-product-compliance
Lightning Source LLC
LaVergne TN
LVHW022107200926
848481LV00003B/1083
9781916698741